Crime ... ce 1945

Making Contemporary Britain

General Editor: Anthony Seldon
Consultant Editor: Peter Hennessy

Published

Northern Ireland since 1968
Paul Arthur and Keith Jeffery

British General Elections since 1945
David Butler

Britain and the Suez Crisis
David Carlton

British Defence since 1945
Michael Dockrill

Britain and the Falklands War
Lawrence Freedman

Consensus Politics from Attlee to Thatcher
Dennis Kavanagh and Peter Morris

Crime and Criminal Justice since 1945
Terence Morris

Forthcoming

British Industry since 1945
Margaret Ackrill

Electoral Change since 1945
Ivor Crewe

The End of Empire
John Darwin

The Attlee Government
Peter Hennessy

Race Relations since 1945
Zig Layton-Henry

Britain and the Korean War
Callum Macdonald

The Mass Media
Colin Seymour-Ure

Government and the Unions
Robert Taylor

Terrorism
Paul Wilkinson

British Public Opinion
Robert Worcester

Institute of Contemporary British History
34 Tavistock Square, London WCIH 9EZ

Crime and Criminal Justice since 1945

Terence Morris

Basil Blackwell

First published 1989

Basil Blackwell Ltd
108 Cowley Road, Oxford, OX4 1JF, UK

Basil Blackwell Inc.
432 Park Avenue South, Suite 1503
New York, NY 10016, USA

British Library Cataloguing in Publication Data

Morris, Terence, *1931–*
Crime and criminal justice since 1945
(Making contemporary Britain).
1. Great Britain. Crime & punishment, 1945–1988
I. Title II. Series
364'.941
ISBN 0–631–16108–2
ISBN 0–631–16109–0 Pbk

Library of Congress Cataloging in Publication Data

Morris, Terence.
Crime and criminal justice since 1945.
(Making contemporary Britain)

Bibliography: p.
Includes index.
1. Criminal justice, Administration of –
Great Britain. I. Title II. Series.
HV9960.G7M68 1989 364'.941 88–7719
ISBN 0–631–16108–2
ISBN 0–631–16109–0

Typeset in 11 on 12.5 pt Ehrhardt
by Setrite Typesetter
Printed in Great Britain by Billing & Sons Ltd, Worcester

Contents

For Louis:
truly, a man among lawyers

General Editor's Preface

The Institute of Contemporary British History's series *Making Contemporary Britain* is aimed directly at students in schools and universities and at others interested in learning more about topics in post-war British history. In the series, authors are less attempting to break new ground than presenting clear and balanced overviews of the state of knowledge on each of the topics.

The ICBH was founded in October 1986 with the objective of promoting the study of British history since 1945 at every level. To that end, it publishes books and a quarterly journal, *Contemporary Record*; it organizes seminars and conferences for school students, undergraduates, researchers and teachers of post-war history; and it runs a number of research programmes and other activities.

A central theme of the ICBH's work is that post-war history is too often neglected in British schools, institutes of higher education and beyond. The ICBH acknowledges the validity of the arguments against the study of recent history, notably the problems of bias, of overly subjective teaching and writing, and the difficulties of perspective. But it believes that the values of studying post-war history outweigh the drawbacks, and that the health and future of a liberal democracy require that its citizens know more about the most recent past of their country than the limited knowledge possessed by British citizens, young and old, today. Indeed, the ICBH believes that the dangers of political indoctrination are higher where the young are *not* informed of the recent past.

The subject of Terence Morris's book is given particular piquancy by the widespread contemporary concern about crime, the criminal justice system and policing methods. According to one source (Ralf Dahrendorf, 1985), violent crime and theft in Britain has tripled or quadrupled since the 1960s. Part of this increase is certainly due to a greater incidence of the *reporting* of crime, as Morris shows. But much of it is due to an increase in the incidence of crime, with especial concern being youth and drug-induced crime.

The author provides one of the first overviews of the subject during the post-war period. He shows that there was a consensus in the approaches of Labour and Conservative governments in their criminal justice policy which lasted until the early 1970s. From that period on, he argues, the New Right caught on to law and order as a political issue, and in doing so seized the initiative. He shows how the right successfully linked law and order questions, including trade union and public order disturbances, to its whole domestic policy and has developed an opening for the policy of privatization in this area of near total state monopoly hitherto. The Labour party, in contrast, tried to defend the pragmatic rehabilitation position with a conspicuous lack of success.

The book is perhaps more partisan than some in the series. Not everyone will share Morris's viewpoint. The breakdown of the consensus has indeed forced a polarization of positions, and the author does not conceal where his own preferences lie. The book can be read with profit by all concerned with criminal justice, whether students or practitioners. There has seldom been a time when there has been a greater need for historical understanding and clarity on the subject.

Anthony Seldon

Acknowledgements

The faults, blemishes, defects, omissions and other failings that may be found in this book are, it goes without saying, entirely mine, although I would disavow the use of the 'z' in place of the 's' and other minor barbarities. Left to my own devices, I would prefer that all tickets continued to be shewn by railway travellers, especially by men wearing trowsers. But in putting it together, I am indebted to a number of people who have helped both directly and indirectly with the task.

I am grateful to my acquaintances in the criminal justice system who often share with academics much more than they realize; in particular those policemen of all ranks who have discussed their work openly and have never shrunk from being frank about their perceptions of the problems of crime and the politics of criminal justice. In particular, I should like to thank a number of Chief Constables who have given me, over the past year, quite astonishingly generous amounts of their time. That they should have done so is not only a testimony to their commitment to the concept of 'community policing' in the very widest sense of being open to serious inquirers, but also a comforting reassurance that those who currently guide the police service are still a very long way from espousing the kind of simplistic authoritarianism that would readily make it a servile creature of government.

At LSE I am more than fortunate in having as colleagues David Downes and Paul Rock, dear friends and valued critics, who provide me with an ever present gage of scholarship and intellectual stimulation. My wife Penelope assisted greatly, not only in unravelling more than 40 years of criminal statistics, but in doing so with a patience worthy of her namesake.

Not least there are those who would probably be surprised to learn that they had contributed anything. They include all those judges and magistrates, wise and just, pompous and irascible, to whose words I have listened since my student days as well as that tragic cavalcade of humanity, weak and vicious, sick and unfortunate, whose passage through the courts I have both witnessed and in a sense assisted for more than 20 years.

Terence Morris
Winchester

1 Introduction

In the contemporary world, crime is frequently on the agenda of political debate. In Britain, none of the major parties has been able to avoid some mention of it as a manifesto item in elections during the past decade. As an issue, it probably first became prominent in the United States of America where it was espoused by elements on the political right, and this phenomenon has been paralleled in Western Europe, notably in France but even in The Netherlands which tends to pursue the most relaxed attitude towards these matters of any country in the European Community.[1] The issue, having been raised by the right, has had to be addressed by those at the other end of the political spectrum, but the response has not always been either consistently coherent or comparably aggressive; indeed, the situation has mirrored that in politics generally where the right, especially the conspicuously successful right, as represented by Reaganism and Thatcherism, has challenged what was previously the received wisdom without producing a convincing counter-challenge from the opposition. Just as in economic theory monetarism of the kind promoted by Milton Friedman became ascendant over that of Keynes, so in the criminal justice field theories of 'incapacitation' and 'containment' successfully displaced those of 'rehabilitation' and reform. The comparison is not entirely straightforward, for the rejection of Keynesian economics has had more to do with an ideological distaste for political programmes that assume the desirability both of stimulating the economy through public expenditure and of providing a system of universal welfare benefit through direct taxation than any overt failure of Keynesian theory in practice.[2] The rehabilitative ideal in criminal justice was becoming the subject of scepticism not only about its effectiveness but also about its moral propriety some while before the promoters of 'law and order' began to enthuse over the ideas of 'incapacitation' and 'containment' that arose from theorists of the 'justice' school of penal philosophy in the 1970s. In brief, the evidence for the failure of rehabilitation to solve the problem of crime is substantially stronger than that on which Keynesian economics may be justly condemned as unfitted to solve the economic problems of the contemporary world.

What is crime?

These are themes that will be discussed elsewhere in this book, but at this stage it may be helpful to spend a little time considering just what it is we are talking about when we use the words 'crime' and 'criminal'. In simple terms, a crime is an action – or omission – which is the subject of some part of the criminal law and is punishable by the state. A crime must be distinguished from a 'civil wrong', a matter that gives rise to an action in law but on the part of an aggrieved party against someone else who is alleged to have caused the injury. Thus, for example, if A throws a brick through the front window of B's house, A commits the offence of criminal damage for which he may be tried by a criminal court, convicted and punished. On the other hand, if B neglects to keep the roof of his house in good repair with the result that one day a slate comes off and strikes A as he is passing in the street below, B has liability in what is known in law as *tort* for the injury he has caused to A through his neglect. A may then take B to the County Court and sue B for damages.

Crimes differ from civil wrongs in two main ways: first, for there to be a crime there must be an *intention*: A *intended* to break B's window and threw the brick for that specific purpose, whereas B was merely negligent in not making sure that the slates on his roof were securely fastened; it was never his *intention* that A, or anyone else, should be injured. Secondly, crimes are defined as offences against the whole community, as represented by the state or, in the case of England, the Crown; while torts or other civil wrongs, like failure to comply with the terms of a contract, are seen as disputes between individual parties; the role of the state through the courts in such cases is that of an arbitrator.

One of the consequences of the distinction is that although the outcome of civil wrongs may be very serious for individuals – for example, being paralysed by an accident arising from another person's negligence – society does not regard the wrongdoer as being particularly 'wicked' or 'bad' in contrast to the person convicted of a crime, however trivial. There is a certain apparent absurdity in this but it springs from the distinction that is made about intention and has very little to do with the actual consequences of the action.[3]

There is, however, a complication in that some actions can be both crimes *and* civil wrongs. For example, a drunken driver who knocks down and seriously injures a cyclist may be convicted of the crime of driving with an excess of alcohol and possibly of the crime of driving recklessly, while at the same time he is liable for damages in civil law for the injury he has caused to the cyclist. The criminal court may fine him or imprison him, probably not more than a few hundred pounds or for more than a few months, but the amount of damages he – or his insurers – may have to pay could amount to tens or even hundreds of thousands of pounds.

There is a constant interplay between the concepts of criminal and civil liability which does not always reflect either what people feel or what they think *ought* to happen to the person who has caused the trouble. It is not perhaps surprising that this should be so and in many non-Western societies these kinds of nice distinctions which are made by Western legal systems scarcely exist. What is more common in such societies is for all 'wrongdoing' to be seen as a matter involving the parties concerned, with the central authority of the community – the chief or tribal elders – acting as arbitrator and source of knowledge about what are the traditions of the community governing redress in such situations.

But to return to our own society: what people tend to worry about is not being hit on the head by loose slates or even being mown down by drunken drivers, but rather being burgled or 'mugged' on a dark street or being the victim of physical violence. Fortunately, fewer people actually experience crime than worry about it, and the facts about crime are often at variance with what people believe to be the state of crime.[4] Not a little of the difficulty springs from the defects of both criminal statistics themselves and their interpretation.

Of all social statistics, those relating to crime are probably among the most inaccurate. Births, marriages and deaths are reported not only because they are important events, but also because those reporting them may have something to lose and frequently something to gain by doing so, such as Child Benefit, tax rebates or insurance payments. Criminal statistics derive from two sources: the reporting of events by members of the public and direct observation of actions by the police. Of the two, the former predominates and this is a primary source of difficulty. For not everyone has the motivation to report an offence; it may be too trivial, it may be inconvenient or embarrassing or it may involve a conflict of loyalties. Offences such as domestic burglary tend to be reported where the householder is insured, but in poor areas where insurance is rare many such crimes go unreported. Indecent sexual exposure and domestic assault, where the victim herself feels the need to draw a veil over the event, may similarly go unreported. Until very recently, this was very much the case with rape; the victim was often subjected to the most humiliating kind of interrogation in order to substantiate the truth of her story.[5]

Thus motivation and disincentive play a critical part in determining the public knowledge of crime, even in its raw dimension. But what is no less important is the way in which illegal actions are classified in the processes of the criminal justice system itself. Suppose an aggressive driver collides with another vehicle and causes an accident; depending upon the consequences, the police may decide not to prosecute, to charge careless driving or charge reckless driving. If someone has died, the charge may be causing death by reckless driving; if alcohol is involved, driving with excess alcohol may also be a possible charge. What the crime 'looks like' when it reaches court depends on a variety of things: the nature of the offence itself, the circumstances and consequences, the character of the offender, including any previous convictions or public profile (for many years no member of the Royal Family was ever prosecuted for a motoring offence) and, not least, whether a bargain may be struck whereby the offender agrees to plead guilty to a lesser charge in return for a more serious one being dropped. Since it is generally the case that prosecutors are more concerned to get a 'result' than to pursue an abstract concept of 'justice', plea bargains and instrumental decisions about whether going for a lesser charge will be more likely to produce the desired 'result' will distort the picture still further. In fact, the greater the procedural 'distance' from the event itself, the less reliable is the definitive account. In the extreme case, a burglar may have certainly broken into a house and stolen some property, but because of a legal technicality or some other inability on the part of the prosecution to prove its case, a conviction is impossible. Strictly speaking, this is a statement that there has been no crime, but in practical terms this is clearly a nonsense. Unless we carry out specialized research, there is no way of distinguishing between acquittals that are genuine, those where the court is uncertain and has given the benefit of any doubt to the offender (as it is required to do) even though the offence was indeed committed and the third category of those who are without the least doubt guilty but who succeed in escaping justice on account of technicalities or the failure of the prosecution to come up with the required evidence.

The sorts of offences that become public knowledge, although they may be individually not very serious, nevertheless belong to categories of crime that society considers to be comparatively grave. Theft, for example, is a grave crime, but a particular theft, say of a ballpoint pen by a child from another's pencil box at school, is not as serious as the theft of someone's wallet in a changing room and certainly not as serious as the theft of one million pounds of gold bullion from a transit shed at London Airport. Yet all involve the same elements that the law has to establish: action and intention. The same may be true of robbery. Some robberies, like those of cash being carried into or out of banks, may involve gross violence and the taking of very large sums of money; other robberies, although they share the same characteristic deployment of physical force or the threat of it, may be on a much smaller scale, including the robbery of a shopkeeper in which only a few pounds are taken from the till right down to the primary school playground hoodlum who robs his classmate of ten pence.

Not all dishonesty is reflected in the criminal statistics. Quite apart from the kind of dishonest practices in commercial life, many of which are the subject of civil rather than criminal proceedings, there are other forms of dishonesty which rarely come to light and then only when the offender is caught. Thus, we have only estimates of how many people actually avoid paying for a television licence or their proper fare on public transport; we only know about those who are actually detected, not least since only the most ill-disposed and vindictive of their fellow citizens are likely to report them. Yet in terms of the morality of behaviour it is hard to draw a defensible distinction between the person who dishonestly travels without paying his fare, sneaking past the ticket collector, and the one who slyly takes a small item of property while the owner is temporarily distracted. Criminal statistics do not provide us with a comprehensive measure of human wickedness; only an indication of the kinds of issues with which the criminal justice system has been concerned at any particular time. Indeed, some criminologists would argue that they tell us more about the activities of law enforcers than about either criminals or the crimes they commit.

Changes in the 'nature' of crime

Crime, as the law defines it, is a much less static concept than most people suppose. The law of homicide, governing such things as murder, manslaughter and infanticide, has changed a great deal since Victorian times and enormously since the Middle Ages, having undergone processes of refinement in response to both changes in moral outlook and scientific knowledge about human behaviour, especially of those whom we now identify as mentally disordered. Other 'crimes', like those dealing with the practice of witchcraft and sorcery have disappeared altogether from the statute book because people no longer accept the existence of the devil or the possibility of influencing events by magic.[6] Homosexual activity between consenting adults ceased to be a crime in 1967.[7] On the other hand, new crimes have appeared that arise specifically from the conditions and requirements of modern life, almost all of them of a regulatory nature and backed by the ultimate sanctions of the criminal law. And there are examples of 'new' crimes that have been defined in consequence of changed attitudes over the years towards, for example, women, children and animals, who in past times endured suffering and exploitation that was accepted as normal. Although many of the changes that have occurred have come about as a result of new evaluations of what is socially and morally important, it would be a mistake to assume that they have been met with universal enthusiasm or acceptance. For although most people would agree that there is no longer any strong case for prosecuting witches or depressed people who attempt to kill themselves, not everyone was in favour of making male homosexuality tolerable between consenting adults. Currently, and no doubt stimulated in part by the fear of AIDS, there is great hostility towards homosexuals and the 'promotion' of homosexuality by local government authorities is now illegal.[8] And where animals are concerned, there is a serious body of opinion that argues that existing laws are grossly inadequate to protect animals from suffering in the course of laboratory experiments or from being hunted to death for pleasure in what are called 'field sports'.

Differing views about what ought to be 'criminal'

In contrast to many simpler societies and what obtained in a much earlier period of English history, there are strong elements of moral pluralism in contemporary Britain. It has recently become fashionable to think of the 1960s as an era of 'permissiveness' that eroded a sterner and more uniformly accepted set of values and behavioural patterns that had held sway before then. The reality is somewhat different. Serious political dissent, involving strong views about the ownership of property and the exercise of power, manifested itself in the seventeenth century and was a major element in the English Civil War, while the Rationalism of the eighteenth century and the writings of Voltaire and Rousseau had an immense influence on the development of a popular radicalism that in turn helped to shape the course of events in Victorian England. Similarly, the revival of Christianity at this time, especially in its Nonconformist and Evangelical forms, seriously challenged many of the conventions of *laissez-faire* capitalism, such as the exploitation of women and children in factories and mines and of slaves in the West India plantations. The movement had important consequences for new legislation. In the nineteenth century there were disputes about the propriety of birth control, atheism, the control of prostitution, capital punishment, the rights of women, the position of trade unions and much else besides. It is a grave mistake to confuse the seemingly monolithic face of a public morality promoted by powerful agencies of social control such as the established church, the courts and the great professions of medicine and the law – to say nothing of the respected political figures of the day – for a popular uniformity of belief transformed into behaviour. Behind the publicly projected images of society there has always been an alternative of dissent. Some dissenters sought to 'liberate' themselves and others from conventions – very often sexual conventions – that they held to be undesirably oppressive but risked the sanctions of the law in doing so. In the area of family planning, Charles Bradlaugh and Annie Besant were prosecuted and Marie Stopes came close to it.[9] The works of D. H. Lawrence[10] and James Joyce could not originally be published without fear of criminal prosecution, and some of Jacob Epstein's sculpture was held to be obscene. In contrast, until this century there were no laws against taking drugs for pleasure, including those derived from opium.

There is, in effect, a substantial degree of moral pluralism in British society and it has been around for a long time. It is almost certainly the combination of the growth of popular education and an improvement in the media of mass communications (to a degree that even our grandparents would have thought incredible) that have revealed the extent of the heterogeneity of values and beliefs. Given, too, the increasing cultural diversity of Britain resulting from the presence of new ethnic minorities, it may be soon impossible to identify little more than a set of core values to serve as a fairly narrow base upon which to construct any kind of moral consensus.

What all this means is that we have to be extremely careful before we assume that 'crime' – and the official public response to it – has an objective meaning that can ignore the differences of age and sex, class and ethnicity. Theft in an inner-city ghetto may be viewed very differently by the unemployed teenage thief and the magistrate or judge who sentences him. The former may see the matter as a 'normal' part of life, and share none of the sense of moral outrage felt by the latter. The judge or magistrate, for his or her part, may be acquainted with a fellow member of the golf club recently convicted of drunken driving or a property developer who has sailed too close to the wind in his business dealings. Different moral constituencies will evaluate these things differently.[11]

A great deal of what we understand about the social world, including crime, is mediated through the agency of radio, television and the press. Radio and television, although generally maintaining high standards of impartial objectivity in reporting, must of necessity be selective since news bulletins are severely restricted by time. Where the newspapers are concerned, there are no comparable restrictions on the length of treatment but standards of objectivity and impartiality are more variable. While the 'quality' newspapers may be restrained in their language, there may be no significant limits on the expression of partisan points of view. At the 'popular' end of the market partisanship is, if anything, brazenly proclaimed and partiality of viewpoint is often expressed through a consciously deliberate use of a demotic hyperbole.[12]

Changes in the communication of information and ideas

During the period covered in this book, the character and influence of the mass media of communication have undergone far-reaching and fundamental changes. Not only has the nature of journalism changed but the virtual monopoly of BBC radio has been challenged not only by television, but by commercial broadcasting in both media. The press, too, has undergone a sea change. There are fewer newspapers than 40 years ago, and the number of newspaper proprietors has diminished while their individual power has grown. Increasingly, in the past decade, the majority of the press has aligned itself not only with the politics of the New Right, but with a view of social issues that perceives crime as a major evil that cannot be too much suppressed; the corollary of that view is an illiberal interpretation of objective attempts to analyse the phenomenon of crime and devise positive remedies for it. In consequence, not a few people in Britain have grave fears about the extent and character of crime that are often ill founded in fact. They may hold views about the choice of solutions to the problem that are more in accord with the retributive nature of European penology before the time of the great reformers, Howard, Bentham and Beccaria, whose ideas sprang from the rich soil of the eighteenth-century Enlightenment. On the other hand, there is evidence that many others are less punitively retributive in their views than stories in the press would suggest.[13]

In the following discussion of 'crime', then, these considerations should be at the back of the reader's mind. And where reference is made in this book to the official statistics of crime there will be no need to restate the proposition that crime is among the most deceptive of social phenomena, since even those instances where it appears presented in ways that are at their most objective and scientific can be extremely misleading. Crime, it must also be remembered, arises not simply from legal categorizations of behaviour but from social processes. The phenomenon of law-breaking is social in that both the opportunities for it and the responses to it occur within a framework of social action, even where the original motivation may lie deep in the recesses of the human psyche. As societies change, so do the patterns of crime, and by the same token the continuities of social life reproduce continuities of criminal behaviour from one age to the next. For this reason, any account of crime and the responses to it in post-war Britain has to take into account many of the things that have happened in British society since the war, some of which may seem at first sight to be of only passing significance or even irrelevant. Independently of individual human motivation, it is still possible to speak of what the nineteenth-century Belgian statistician Adolphe Quetelet called a 'budget' of crime: 'Society bears in its womb the embryo of every crime that will be committed. It prepares for crime, so to speak, while the criminal is merely the tool.'[14]

Notes

1 See David Downes, *Contrasts in Tolerance: Post-War Penal Policies in the Netherlands and England and Wales* (Oxford, Oxford University Press, 1988). The Scandinavian countries have pursued liberal penal policies for very many years and have often been regarded as a bench-mark of progressive practice.

2 Keynesian theory was conspicuously successful in reinvigorating the American economy from 1932 onwards during Roosevelt's 'New Deal'. It was almost axiomatic in post-war economic policy in Britain, at least until the late 1960s.

3 If a couple of young boys, trespassing in a railway siding, climb into a coach and, while playing with matches, set it on fire, they may do a very considerable amount of damage. But the consequences of their childish, if dangerous, prank cannot be said to stem from any deep-seated intention, still less, foreknowledge. For this reason, juvenile delinquents are often treated more like civil wrongdoers than adult criminals.

4 See *The British Crime Survey*, Home Office Research Study, no. 76 (London, HMSO, 1983); *Victims of Crime: the Dimensions of Risk*, Home Office Research Study, no. 81 (London, HMSO, 1984) and *Fear of Crime in England and Wales*, Home Office Research Study, no. 78 (London, HMSO, 1984).

5 A television programme made with the cooperation of the Thames Valley Police in 1982 was almost certainly the turning point in improving the treatment of rape victims by the police.

6 Under Acts of 1541 and 1603 witchcraft was punishable by death. The last executions for witchcraft in England, that of a woman and her daughter (aged nine), took place by hanging in 1716. The 'reforming' Witchcraft Act of 1735 was repealed by the Fraudulent Mediums Act 1951.

7 A nationally publicized trial involving a number of men, including a peer of the realm, in the mid-1950s led to the establishment of the Wolfenden Committee which, charged with examining the law with regard to both homosexuality and prostitution, recommended important changes in the law. These were significantly more advantageous to homosexuals than to prostitutes (*Report of the Departmental Committee on Homosexuality and Prostitution*, London, HMSO, 1957, Cmnd 247).

8 See Clause 28 of the Local Government Bill published in 1987.

9 Charles Bradlaugh, an atheist who refused to swear an oath when elected to the House of Commons, lived with Annie Besant to whom he could not be married as his first wife was still alive, though a deteriorated alcoholic. In 1877 they republished

Knowlton's *Fruits of Philosophy*, an early nineteenth-century tract on contraception. Dr Marie Stopes, the foundress of modern family planning in Britain, came close to having her book *Married Love* (1918) defined as an obscene libel and became embroiled in a long, acrimonious and punitively ruinous libel action with Dr Halliday Sutherland, a medical practitioner who supported the position then held by the Roman Catholic church. She eventually lost.

10 The case of *R.* v. *Penguin Books Ltd*, following the publication of an unexpurgated version of D. H. Lawrence's *Lady Chatterley's Lover* in 1960, was a milestone in the relaxation of censorship (see chapter 8).

11 A remark, frequently attributed to Berthold Brecht, poses the question; 'What is the crime of robbing a bank compared with the crime of owning one?' A not dissimilar sentiment is expressed by Robert Allerton, a professional thief, in Tony Parker's *The Courage of his Convictions* (London, Heinemann, 1962).

12 The language of the popular press tends towards the hyperbolic. When people disagree, 'rows flare'; a bishop of unorthodox views is not criticized but 'slammed', and so on.

13 See *The British Crime Survey* (London, HMSO, 1983). An opinion survey published at about the same time and conducted jointly by the *Observer* newspaper and the Prison Reform Trust (Stephen Shaw, *The People's Justice*, London PRT, 1982) bears out the contention that many people are less punitive than some newspapers and politicians would have us believe. See also National Association for the Care and Resettlement of Offenders (NACRO), *Public Opinion and Sentencing* (London, NACRO, 1986).

14 Adolphe Quetelet, *Essai de Physique Sociale* (Brussels, 1869).

2 Britain in 1945

Britain in the spring of 1945 was a society both exhausted and exhilarated. The war, which had begun in September 1939 and which was not to end until the surrender of Japan in August 1945, had taken an enormous toll. Unlike the war of 1914–18, in which the civilian population had played a largely passive role, this had been a war in which civilian casualties had been great. In the winter of 1940–1 German bombers had devastated large areas of cities as far apart as London and Glasgow, Liverpool and Southampton; specific so-called 'Baedeker raids' had been made on cathedral towns such as Canterbury and Exeter for no purpose other than to reduce civilian morale.

After 1941, when the *Luftwaffe* had lost superiority in the air through the development of effective radar defence and the major air attacks had ceased, the civilian population still suffered from the privations of rationing in consequence of the success of the German U-boats in sinking the shipping on the North Atlantic which brought in food, fuel and other commodities necessary to sustain an island which was to all intents and purposes under siege. When the Battle of the Atlantic reached its height in 1942 the meat ration was reduced to a mere two ounces per person per week. Under these conditions, the civilian population had to supply the labour for an increased industrial production to satisfy the growing needs of the war effort itself.

But if Britain was exhausted in 1945 it was also exhilarated by the prospect of a brighter future. To understand the significance of this we need to go back, beyond the ecstatic celebrations of VE Day in 1945 when the remnants of the German army surrendered on Luneberg Heath, to the condition of Britain in the decade 1929–39.

Britain before the war

The years following the end of the First World War had been troubled, and society was adjusting to what were radical and irreversible changes. Women were not only politicized but enfranchised and working men began to view the dimensions of political life from a new perspective as a result of their experiences in the Great War. The General Strike of 1926 was the most serious challenge to established order since the Chartists had assembled in 1848. The Wall Street stock market crash of 1929 had far-reaching effects upon the world economy which Britain did not escape. By 1931 the number of unemployed had reached three million, a staggering figure for those days. The effect upon manufacturing industry was catastrophic and was not reversed until it was artificially galvanized into new life in 1940. And although the south-east of the country enjoyed a degree of comparative prosperity during this period, experiencing the growth of service industries and those concerned with the production of consumer goods for a newly emerging lower middle class, the regions remote from London that were the traditional centres of heavy manufacturing, industry and mining bore the brunt of the economic depression. The distinctions between 'north' and 'south' (that had provided a title for Mrs Gaskell's novel) were exacerbated by the Depression, reiterating the themes of the 'two nations' Disraeli had discussed in *Sybil*.

In a curious way, the condition of Britain in the period immediately before the outbreak of war was relatively tranquil, notwithstanding the immense hardships endured not only by the unemployed and their families, but also by those whose wages had been reduced following the 1929–31 crisis.[1] The Labour party, although they had won two general elections (in 1924 and 1929), had never secured a working majority in the House of Commons, and in 1931, following the defeat of the Labour administration, Ramsay Macdonald had formed a National Government. The effect of this was deeply to divide the whole Labour movement, among whom Macdonald was widely regarded as a traitor, and to render it politically ineffective. At the general election in June 1935 the Conservatives were returned to office under the leadership of Baldwin. After 1935, the economy began slowly to recover but it required the supervention of the war to eradicate the effects of unemployment.

Some modern commentators have identified high unemployment with the process of destabilization and *anomie*, leading to the rejection of established social norms and to crime. But much depends upon the identity of the groups affected. The principal difference between the three million unemployed in 1931 and the three million unemployed in the late 1980s is of just such an order.[2] The inter-war period was characterized *par excellence* by the 'one child – no child' family, with the result that children and young people were a far smaller proportion of the population than they are now. Unemployment was experienced by adult males of relatively mature years while young people, on account of low wage rates, were often able to find work. The picture of unemployment before the war, captured in the socially sensitive black and white photography of the time, is of men resigned and apathetic rather than revolutionary.[3] Meanwhile, the Labour movement continued in schism: attempts to form a Popular Front resulted in the expulsion from the party of a number of potentially important figures, notably Sir Stafford Cripps.[4] On the domestic front, the most important event was probably the abdication of Edward VIII in 1936 in consequence of his determination to make a morganatic marriage with the twice-divorced American socialite Wallis Simpson. Cynical observers remarked upon the importance of the celebrations of the Silver Jubilee of George V in 1935 and the Coronation of George VI in 1937 as instances of 'bread and circuses' that distracted from reality.[5]

It would be wrong, however, to describe the 1930s as a period of total social tranquillity. Public disorders were not unknown, either of an industrial or a political nature, but they tended to be limited and specific to time and place. Undoubtedly the most serious were the troubles in London's East End in 1935 and 1936 involving the British Union of Fascists (BUF). Sir Oswald Mosley, a brilliant if mercurial figure, had, as a socialist, been Chancellor of the Duchy of Lancaster in Macdonald's 1931 administration but by 1934 he had fallen under the spell of Hitler and had formed the BUF. Like the National Socialist Party in Germany, the BUF made anti-semitism one of its focal concerns and young men – often unemployed – eagerly donned their Nazi-style uniforms and emulated their continental counterparts in intimidating Jews on the street and damaging Jewish shops and synagogues. The Communists, who had a strong following in the East End,[6] not only defended themselves when the BUF attempted to break up their meetings but engaged with the 'blackshirts' as they came to be known in street fighting. Although these troubles were localized, they were of sufficient importance for Parliament to pass the Public Order Act of 1936 which, among other things, banned the wearing of military-style uniforms by members of political parties.[7] The Fascist movement, though constrained, did not entirely disappear, notwithstanding that Mosley and his colleagues were detained under Regulation 18(b) at the outbreak of war. *Action*, the party's newspaper with its striking 'flash and circle' logo, was still circulating in the winter of 1939–40 with accounts of how the war had been engineered by the 'Wall Street yiddy boys'. The movement reappeared after the war focusing not on anti-semitism but upon 'coloured' immigration.[8]

Crime, other than public disorder, was not a noticeable feature of pre-war society.[9] Although the number of crimes reported to the police had been steadily rising since the 1920s, the numbers were still small compared with those of today. In 1938, for example, there were only 283,220 serious offences of all kinds known to the police in England and Wales compared with a current figure that is in excess of three million. Of those offences in 1938 the police managed to 'clear up' marginally over 50 per cent compared with a contemporary figure of about 32 per cent.[10] Nor were the numbers of offenders before the courts particularly large. In 1935 the rate per 100,000 of all those over the age of 17 convicted of serious offences in all courts was only 148; by 1951 this had risen to 259. The kinds of offences which cause public anxiety today were comparatively rare. Crimes of violence against the person – excluding homicide and rape – averaged just under 2,000 annually for the period

1930–9, while burglaries averaged just under 40,000 a year and thefts of motor vehicles were too few to be separately recorded in criminal statistics and were lumped together with thefts of pedal cycles and other simple and minor larcenies.

Far from being overcrowded, prisons were actually being closed down. The reason for this was that greater use was being made of non-custodial sentences, notably probation orders which, although available in law as a sentence to the courts since 1908, had not developed on account of the fact that few courts had taken the trouble to appoint probation officers until 1925 when it became compulsory to do so. Considerable changes were also taking place within the prison system, the most striking of which was the introduction of 'open' institutions. The first was an 'open' borstal for young offenders at Lowdham in Nottinghamshire in 1931 and the second New Hall Camp, an open prison near Wakefield in Yorkshire.

Britain in wartime

One of the immediate effects of the war was to lessen the social deprivation that had blighted the lives of the least privileged in the preceding decade; almost everyone who could work had the opportunity to do so and, indeed, such was the shortage of labour that eventually women who were without family responsibilities were conscripted into war work by the Ministry of Labour. Industry itself was soon brought under centralized government direction and, although there was a legal prohibition on strikes,[11] the appointment of Ernest Bevin, the most powerful trade union leader of the day, to the War Cabinet in 1940 ensured that the rewards of labour in the war effort would be generous.

A consequence of this was a potentially large volume of money available for consumer demand just at the time when the production of consumer goods was being severely restricted. Various devices were employed to mop up this surplus. A sales tax known as Purchase Tax was applied to what were deemed luxury goods[12] and additional income tax was deducted for which certificates were issued known as Post-War Credits.[13] The lesson having been learned from the First World War, rationing of food had been introduced in January 1940; petrol rationing ensured strictly limited supplies to those with essential needs, and gradually almost everything, including clothing and washing soap, required a ration coupon. Many goods were available only in a standard 'utility' form and bore a mark or label with the logo 'CC41'. But one of the consequences of the conjunction of rationing and an increase in effective consumer demand was the development of the black market. The study of the black market has almost certainly been a lost criminological opportunity and only Mannheim seems to have looked at it and other wartime offences with anything more than a passing interest.[14]

What is interesting about the black market is that it involved not only the kinds of people who would, in the ordinary course of events, be involved in shady dealings on the margins of the law, but large numbers of middle-class people who would never have considered themselves criminals in the commonly understood sense of the term. Thus, cleaning women often and willingly sold their clothing coupons for cash ensuring that their middle-class employers could still dress *à la mode* and, while food ration coupons were less negotiable, the cash bribery of butchers and grocers was commonplace in order to secure extra weight or the better cuts of meat. Not infrequently, however, the bribery was in the form of cigarettes which were also often in short supply.[15] Prosecutions for black market offences were comparatively rare and the sentence of six months' imprisonment on Ivor Novello in 1943 for driving a car with black market petrol was a national noted event.[16]

The Defence Regulations had provided, in extreme cases, for the death penalty in cases involving the looting of property vulnerable as a result of enemy action. The situation only occurred during the major period of bombing in the winter of 1940–1 but there were, nevertheless, numerous instances of both shops and residential properties that had been damaged or made otherwise vulnerable being plundered. In the event, the death penalty was never imposed, although numbers of prison sentences were, some of them quite severe. These court proceedings were seldom reported widely – and sometimes not all – because the situation was somewhat embarrassingly complicated by the fact that almost all the offenders were either civil defence personnel or War Reserve policemen.[17]

Apart from these crimes arising specifically from the situation of wartime and involving people who would otherwise never have been in any trouble, two other wartime conditions contributed to a change in the level of crime. The first of these was the 'black-out'. In order to make navigation and target identification as difficult as possible for the *Luftwaffe*, from the night of 3 September 1939 until the end of the war in Europe it was illegal to show any light in the open during the hours of darkness. There were some relaxations to this; severely masked headlamps on vehicles and very low level lighting on buses, trams and trains was permitted. Bicycles were allowed to use low-powered lamps and pedestrians could use similarly low-powered torches. All such lights had to be extinguished after an air-raid warning. All forms of street lighting and advertisement illumination were totally prohibited and all interior lights in buildings had to be masked by opaque coverings.

The effect of the black-out was to reduce life after dark to something rather akin to life in the Middle Ages, and opportunistic criminals were not slow to take advantage of the situation. Burglaries of domestic and commercial properties increased, as did personal assaults and, although there was an addition to police manpower in the form of the War Reserve and the Special Constabulary, police patrols were hampered by the same conditions that advantaged the criminal.

A second wartime condition was the presence of large numbers of men under arms in the midst of a civilian population. Contingents of enlisted men from Canada began to arrive in 1940, as did Poles, Frenchmen and others escaping from France after Dunkirk. Then, after 1943, increasingly large numbers of American servicemen began to arrive in preparation for the invasion of north-west Europe the following year. Down the centuries, in every army, there have always been men at the margins of social conformity and the situation in the Second World War was no exception. Deserters on the run had perforce to live by crime and often violently.[18] Soldiers out of barracks have always sought their entertainment in ale houses and the company of women, and alcohol-related crimes, such as physical and specifically sexual assaults, could and sometimes did result. The situation was probably amplified by the fact that in wartime the normal standards of behaviour and restraint are not infrequently suspended in the context of the belief that life itself is uncertain; one might be killed by a bomb later that night or one might be posted overseas, never to return.

A fully accurate picture of crime in wartime Britain is probably now beyond our reach, not least since the police had many other things to engage their attention than the precise recording of complaints of crime. The military authorities not infrequently took care of their own malefactors – American personnel were invariably dealt with by their own military police and courts martial.[19] Although most murders probably came to light, it is likely that many rapes did not and while soldiers, especially foreign soldiers,[20] were often the subject of suspicion, we have no clear idea of the relative contribution to crime of servicemen and civilians.

Nor did the prison system escape the effects of war. Throughout the 1930s the Prison Commissioners had pursued many enlightened schemes for reform and development and much had been invested in a Criminal Justice Bill in 1938, the passage of which was terminated by the impending outbreak of war. In 1939 the borstal service, which had been the Commissioners' 'flagship' enterprise, was effectively closed down; the boys were released on licence and the staff, those who did not enlist, were redeployed elsewhere in the prison service. The Defence Regulation 18(b) provided for the detention without trial of aliens and those suspected of being likely to assist the enemy with the result that in the last months of 1939 and well into the summer of 1940 numbers of refugees from Europe, including numerous Jews, were initially detained in prison until they could be screened. To their numbers were added key figures in the British Union of Fascists including Mosley, whose sympathies for Hitler and Mussolini had never been disguised. By a bitter irony of fate, fascists and Jewish refugees from Nazism found themselves confined together for a while in Pentonville.[21]

The prison system had to cope both with reduced manpower and the increased demands of the courts. In the immediate pre-war years the daily average population of prisons in England

and Wales had been between 10,000 and 11,000; by 1945, it was not far short of 15,000, an increase of about 50 per cent in five years.[22]

The climate of optimism

In 1945 there was a substantial popular belief that, unlike what had happened after 1918, when the returning soldiers had had an expectation of a 'Land fit for Heroes' which was soon turned to ashes, this time things were going to be different. To appreciate this feeling it is necessary to understand what had been happening on the commanding heights of government during the war. Churchill, who had replaced Chamberlain in 1940, was a leader plucked not from the front rank of the Conservative party but from the political wilderness; he had not been one of the men of Munich. Although now Conservative by inclination, he had been not only a Liberal but a Liberal minister before 1914 when major social reform was in the air. He understood the importance not only of taking into account the critical role of the working classes in the war effort but also of taking into government figures from the Labour movement who would ensure that they 'delivered'. For this reason, he took on Ernest Bevin and in the course of the war, he took other Labour politicians into the Cabinet. Besides Attlee, he recruited Herbert Morrison, who had been running the London County Council since 1934, Hugh Dalton, Arthur Greenwood and Stafford Cripps. At the same time, there were a number of new recruits into the Civil Service who were to play a crucial role in influencing government thinking, among them William Beveridge and John Maynard Keynes. The conduct of the war, as far as the management of the economy was concerned, was characterized by a kind of planned collectivism that was a new experience and a highly successful one. Its corollary was a set of plans for the period that would immediately follow the cessation of war. Three proposals of immense significance emerged.

First in time was the Beveridge Report. It had begun in 1941 as an inquiry into social insurance. When it emerged in 1943 its scope had been enlarged to cover a comprehensive scheme for dealing with poverty which Beveridge held would only work if there were to be family allowances, a national health service and full employment.[23] The second, which was translated into legislation by 1944, was the reform of education. The Butler Act transformed educational opportunity for a generation of working- and lower middle-class children in the secondary field, which in turn was to lead on to the expansion of the universities in the 1960s. The third was the 1944 White Paper on employment policy which established full employment as a *desideratum* of economic policy.

Of the three proposals, it was the Beveridge Report that fired the popular imagination; it gave some substance to the hope that at the end of *this* war things would indeed be different. The Butler Education Act was to be longer in having its full effect, but the commitment to full employment was to have a profound influence on the shape of British society in the immediate post-war period. As the war came to an end, so the country became alive to the political possibilities of peace. Churchill was confident that a nation that had entrusted to him leadership in war would accord the same trust in peace. Throughout June 1945 his powerful portrait appeared over a poster enjoining the electorate to 'Vote National'.[24] By July, when the overseas service votes had been counted, it became clear that he had lost. Not only had the Conservative party been cut to shreds but the Liberal party had been all but annihilated as had almost every independent and minority interest. Labour, for the first time, had a working majority and of no fewer than 146 seats.

The impact of the election was to spread alarm and despondency among some of the more wealthy and privileged; some spoke as if wholesale confiscation of wealth and the introduction of Soviet-style Communism were imminent. But for the mass of the population, not least the returning servicemen who had elected Labour to power, theirs was the confident expectation that by 'all pulling together' a new society would be built in which not only would Beveridge's 'giants' lie forever silent and vanquished, but full employment and social planning would ensure at last a future for ordinary people in which, to borrow the words of John Ruskin 80 years before, all would be 'well housed, clothed, fed and educated'.[25]

Not only had the social disciplines of wartime convinced people that with proper leadership the seemingly impossible might be accomplished – whether this be the provision of decent housing or full employment – but something of the social philosophy of 'progress' had filtered down into popular thinking.[26] The theorists of progress held that as the material conditions of social life improved, and squalor, poverty and disease became less and less a feature of human existence, so the moral condition of mankind would improve, not least in respect of the way in which it behaved towards its fellows.

It is difficult to say just how far the theory achieved widespread acceptance, but what was true was that increasingly throughout the post-war period it seemed to be disproved. How was it, people asked, that in spite of improved housing, better education, full employment, a comprehensive health service and a social security system that had banished poverty, crime continued to increase? For almost a hundred years a correlation between deprivation and crime had been assumed, yet in spite of material improvement and the abolition of 'want' crime continued to be omnipresent.

Notes

1 The reduction of service pay led to a mutiny in the fleet at Invergordon, the most serious to have occurred in the British Navy since that at the Nore in 1797. The Board of Guardians in the East End also refused to administer lower rates of public assistance.

2 These figures are used in an approximate sense. There is, in fact, considerable debate about the true figure of unemployed persons depending upon how the term 'unemployed' is defined and the reallocation of individuals from the unemployment register to other categories of welfare benefit.

3 Hilda Jennings, in her book *Brynmawr* (London, Allenson and Co., 1934), gives an illuminating account of a social project in South Wales designed to lift a local group from its torpor into some form of positive community-based activity.

4 Cripps, an outstanding lawyer, was invited to join the wartime government by Churchill in 1942 and emerged as Chancellor of the Exchequer in the Attlee administration in 1947, playing a

critical role in the implementation of the strategy for economic recovery. Publicly associated with the ensuing era of consumer austerity, he was, in private life, a man of almost monkish asceticism.

5 The left-wing journalist, Claud Cockburn, managed to unfurl a banner from an upper window in Fleet Street as the carriage of George V and Queen Mary was on its way to St Paul's in full view of the cameras of the newsmen. It read, simply, '25 years of hunger and war'.

6 The last Communist MP, Phil Piratin, was elected in 1945 for the Mile End Division of Stepney. He left the House of Commons in 1950.

7 The Act remained in force until replaced by the Public Order Act of 1986.

8 There is some substance in the view that the BUF can be properly regarded as the lineal ancestor of the National Front. Certainly, the new generation of booted skinheads seem to read *Bulldog* as avidly as their forebears scanned the pages of *Action*.

9 Easily the best account is contained in Hermann Mannheim's, *Social Aspects of Crime in England between the Wars* (London, Allen and Unwin, 1940).

10 *Criminal Statistics for England and Wales* (London, HMSO, annually).

11 Order 1305 of the wartime Defence Regulations had been used in an attempt to end a strike at the Bettshanger colliery in the Kent coalfield in 1943. It had been a failure; even after the strike leaders had been imprisoned in Canterbury gaol, it continued in their absence. It was again unsuccessfully used in 1949 in an attempt to end the London dock strike that was jeopardizing exports. The striking dockers were acquitted by the jury and carried shoulder high from the Old Bailey to the great embarrassment of the government. A contrast might be made with the contemporary legal machinery for dealing with strikes which is indefeasibly successful in that it eschews the manufacture of political martyrs and employs the infinitely more powerful weapon of the sequestration of union funds. Sir Hartley Shawcross, the Attorney General of the time, would never have needed to be vulnerable to the unpredictable vagaries of a jury had such legislation been available.

12 The definition was sufficiently broad as to include such items as fountain pen ink. As a sales tax it continued until the introduction of VAT and its vestigial remnant is to be found in the present tax on new cars.

13 Tardiness on the part of the Treasury in their repayment after

the war was a frequent complaint by those hostile to the Attlee government.

14 See Hermann Mannheim, *Group Problems in Crime and Punishment* (London Routledge and Kegan Paul, 1955).

15 Phrases like 'How about 20 Players and a Number Eight battery?' when used by wartime comedians would produce roars of convulsive laughter from their audiences.

16 The imprisonment of Novello was regarded as especially shocking, not only on account of his being made an example, but because of his record of writing patriotic songs. As a prodigy during the First World War, he had composed no less a ballad than *Keep the Home Fires Burning*.

17 See Hermann Mannheim, *Group Problems in Crime and Punishment*, pp. 102–4.

18 The notorious 'cleft chin' murder in 1945 involved an American deserter and his 18-year-old British girlfriend. At the end of a series of robberies in which she would act as a decoy, a London taxi driver was shot dead. The deserter was hanged but his accomplice subsequently reprieved and released after ten years in prison. Sir Harold Scott estimated that there were 20,000 deserters living off their wits in London in 1946. See David Ascoli, *The Queen's Peace* (London, Hamish Hamilton, 1979).

19 Numbers of servicemen were executed in military prisons during the war. The prison at Shepton Mallet in Somerset which had been abandoned by the Prison Commissioners in 1934 was the place of execution for a number of British personnel. A Canadian Indian soldier, Auguste Sangret, convicted of the murder of Joan Wolfe in 1942, spent longer awaiting execution than any other murderer in modern British legal history and was finally hanged at Wandsworth Prison in 1943. American military policemen, on account of their striking white webbing equipment and white steel helmets, were known as 'snowdrops'.

20 Particularly unpleasant stories circulated about the Poles, almost certainly as a result of the classic amplification of rumour, half-truth and falsehood.

21 Most of the BUF detainees were transferred to detention facilities on the Isle of Man where most remained until about the end of 1943. Refugees, once screened, were fairly rapidly settled in the community. Those Nazi sympathizers who had gone abroad to Germany at the outbreak of war had a less comfortable time. William Joyce, known to wartime audiences as 'Lord Haw Haw' on account of his somewhat nasal patrician accent when he broadcast for the Germans on the same wavelength as the BBC

Home Service, and John Amery were tried for treason at the end of the war and hanged at Pentonville and Wandsworth respectively.

22 *Annual Reports of the Commissioner of Prison for England and Wales: 1920–1938* (London, HMSO).

23 Beveridge identified five 'giants' that had to be slain: Ignorance, Want, Squalor, Idleness and Disease.

24 It is significant that he sought to continue to project a collective rather than a partisan political image.

25 John Ruskin, *Time and Tide* Letter xiii.

26 L.T. Hobhouse, born in 1864 and Martin White Professor of Sociology at the London School of Economics from 1907 to 1929, perhaps the most influential political and social writer in this field.

3 The State of Crime in Post-war Britain

In 1945 the problem of crime did not engage the attention of the public in the way in which it does today. It was not regarded as a political issue in the sense that it had an important place on the agenda of party politics. Rather, it was a kind of backdrop to everyday life. It did not touch as many people as it does today and it would have been difficult to see precisely what kind of partisan gloss could have been put on the matter. In the years immediately after the war there were other, infinitely more pressing, problems facing government, and the energies of the opposition were largely directed towards criticism of the solutions proposed and put into practice. The predominant atmosphere was that of social reconstruction.

In 1945 there was not only a greater degree of consensus about the canons of social propriety as they related to behaviour but also the dominant morality was both more effectively and more widely asserted. Thus, to have been before a criminal court charged with dishonesty, however trivial, was regarded as socially disgraceful. No employer would have been thought unreasonable for dismissing an employee who had been convicted, even of an offence in no way connected with his work. To be convicted of a crime was, in 'respectable' society, to be socially disgraced; the penalty imposed could only amplify that disgrace and it would be extended, by association, to the family of the offender. The theme of social disgrace through crime was, of course, a well-established feature of Victorian and Edwardian literature. Such classics as *The Railway Children* demonstrated the social consequences of conviction for wives and children and the necessity of 'clearing one's name' in the case of the wrongfully accused.[1] In the case of those rightfully convicted the situation was altogether less promising. To have served a prison sentence, for example, far from 'wiping the slate clean' meant that the ex-prisoner would suffer further handicap. Employers would be very chary of taking on a man with a 'record', and previous convictions would be remembered in the folk history of local communities.[2] The term 'gaolbird' was one in common use to describe someone who had been in trouble with the law, however long before.

In many respects such sentiments were not only uncharitably censorious, since they gave the ex-offender little by way of chance to show that he had made amends, but they were also not infrequently based upon a false estimate of the risks of future offending. Of those men sent to prison for the first time in 1945, 88 per cent had not returned within three years. 'Success' rates of the order of 80–90 per cent were by no means uncommon at this time, even though the proportion of offenders imprisoned for the first time who were without any previous convictions had fallen since the 1930s.[3]

The criminal justice system

The low rate of re-offending and the hitherto blameless character of those who were sent to prison at this period contrasts sharply with the experience of the 1970s and 1980s. The reasons for the difference are, however, a little complicated and are not simply a reflection of the increased criminality of our own time. Although there was considerably less crime than now, once caught up in the processes of criminal justice the outcome was likely to be substantially more serious. The extent of police discretion with regard to whether or not a person would be prosecuted for an alleged offence was restricted to the judgement of an officer above the rank of sergeant in relevant cases.[4]

The judicial system was characterized by an absence of legal aid for defendants without means – except on the most serious charges, such as murder or manslaughter, where there was a primitively inadequate system for the defence of 'poor prisoners' – and an almost wholly untrained magistracy. With the exception of a small number of legally qualified stipendiaries, so called on account of the fact of their being salaried, and who sat alone in courts in large cities, almost all urban and all rural Magistrates' Courts were staffed by Justices of the Peace who were not only untrained and unqualified but were appointed by methods that were more often than not directed towards the bestowing of political reward rather than the search for competence. With a few notable exceptions, neither the competence nor the quality of magisterial justice at this time could be regarded as other than woefully inadequate. While the stipendiaries were often indifferent lawyers, the marked absence of a defence lawyer in so many cases before them meant that their incompetence generally went unchallenged. Absence of legal representation also limited appeals, especially those to the highest courts, where mistakes in law, at least, could be corrected. But the stipendiaries were often men[5] of an authoritarian frame of mind who believed that crime should be punished with severity in order that both the offender and anyone minded to follow his example should be clearly deterred. JPs, in contrast, had no legal training at all and on this count were largely at the mercy of their court clerks who, where the JPs were weak, would often assume so dominant a role that a stranger coming into court could have been forgiven for thinking them to be some species of Grand Inquisitor. Becoming a JP was generally a matter of being well connected politically; the various parties would take turns to put names to the Deputy Lieutenant of the County who in turn would put them to the secret committee over which he presided, the result being transmitted by way of a recommendation to the Lord Chancellor. Each party would thus reward its faithful members by a device which carried considerable social status. Not all those rewarded understood much about the criminal justice system and some were totally unsuited to the task temperamentally.[6] Some JPs held the Commission of the

Peace *ex officio* as the mayors of boroughs. Such a JP might well decide to preside over the bench immediately following his mayoral election.[7]

For the majority of magistrates, lay or stipendiary, the core of the penal system was perceived as imprisonment. It had been so for more than a century and neither professional lawyers, nor those sections of society from which JPs were largely drawn, were much influenced by the penal reform movement. Margery Fry, the magisterial descendant of the great Elizabeth Fry, had been instrumental in founding the Magistrates' Association in 1921, but in 1945 only a very small number of justices were members. They were, in consequence, hardly exposed at all to any kind of critical evaluation of their task, let alone any serious discussion of sentencing policies.

Nor was the situation significantly better in the higher reaches of the judiciary. Chairmen of Quarter Sessions and Borough Recorders were not unlike the stipendiary magistrates. The High Court judges were men who were recruited from an even more select sector of the profession and as often as not a judge would be appointed to the criminal bench who had practised in almost any other branch of the law except crime. The criminal law was widely held to be the least complex specialism in the area of legal studies as a whole, and sentencing was regarded as a worthy admixture of common sense and a sound appreciation of popular sentiment. The result was that the sentencing policies given expression in the higher courts were seldom, if at all, more constructive than those which characterized the Magistrates Courts. Legal education paid no attention whatever to either penal philosophy or sentencing practice; criminology was unknown, and psychology and forensic psychiatry were the objects of deep suspicion. If not always as elegantly expressed, the sentiments of judges were inclined to reflect the views of the Victorian lawyer Fitzjames Stephen who argued: 'I think it highly desirable that criminals should be hated, that the punishments inflicted upon them should be so contrived as to give expression to that hatred.'[8]

A direct consequence of the quality of judicial personnel was that imprisonment was frequently used to deal with offenders who not only had never been in trouble before but who would, for various reasons, be very unlikely to be in trouble again. Where offenders were of limited financial means and were ordered to pay fines, there was a discretion available to the court under legislation dating from 1914 to allow them time to pay. But in some courts either that discretion was not exercised or used in such a way as to make it virtually impossible for the offender to do so in the time; the result was that the alternative – a period of imprisonment *in lieu* – would become effective. Thus a sentence of, say, £5 or seven days would often end in the offender serving seven days in prison.

Non-custodial alternatives tended to be seen as proper only in relatively trivial cases from which category theft, fraud, receiving stolen property and burglary would almost always be excluded. The sorts of offences for which many offenders were imprisoned in 1945 would now be regarded as the natural subject for such disposals as probation or fines, but such sentencing policies had at least one advantage for the prison system. The presence of so large a proportion of first offenders who did not subsequently re-offend almost certainly gave the staff and managers of the prisons and borstals a false sense of the effectiveness of their regimes. The Prison Commissioners certainly believed that a low rate of recidivism was an indication of how successful their methods – which they aimed at making increasingly humane and constructive – were in overcoming the criminal disposition.

In 1945 there were, to all intents and purposes, no constraints on the sentencing practices of the courts except in so far as the law itself set out the legal maxima of imprisonment. It was possible to imprison juveniles over the age of 14, defendants who were not legally represented and first offenders. Today, none of these things can be done except that first offenders, those under 21 and those not represented *may* in certain conditions be imprisoned but only after the court's reasons for so doing have been precisely recorded in writing. As far as appeals were concerned, although they had been possible since 1907, the appellant risked not only getting a *longer* sentence but would not have any time during the appeal counted towards his sentence.[9]

Public attitudes to crime

Public attitudes were more frequently articulated with respect to offenders than to the abstract notion of crime, and there is no evidence that then (or indeed now) particular attitudes were characteristic of any social class or group. In this sense neither authoritarian nor liberal penal sentiments acknowledged any boundaries. While penal reformers were for the most part drawn from a middle-class intelligentsia, their political views could be highly divergent. The post-war President of the Howard League was Lord Templewood, the former Sir Samuel Hoare, and the League was later to have a Labour MP, Sir George Benson, as a chairman. Authoritarian sentiments were equally expressed by middle-class spokesmen but they would often have the tacit support of working-class voters.[10] The Christian church was divided. There were those who were aligned with William Temple, the social reformist Archbishop of Canterbury, who argued for both a more humane prison system and the abolition of capital punishment, and others, like the Revd Ball, sometime chaplain of HM Prison Dartmoor, who argued that the imminent prospect of death provided by capital punishment could often be the source of a man's conversion to Christianity.

Crime and criminals have always had a fascination for law-abiding people, even though they might disapprove of criminal behaviour, and the world of post-war Britain was no exception to this. The film, which was arguably the most powerful medium of entertainment in 1945, the wireless not excepted, frequently portrayed crime in stereotypical terms. A substantial proportion of films in 1945 originated in the United States and among them the so-called 'gangster' movie was commonplace. Such films presented criminals as members of an underworld organized in a highly complex fashion and presided over by characters who imitated the notorious figures of Prohibition days, such as Al Capone and 'Legs' Diamond who ruled over Chicago and New York respectively. The action was generally a symbolic interchange between good and evil, represented by police and criminals. Detective fiction was immensely popular, especially in paperback,[11] and it must be remembered that at a time when television was non-existent (transmissions were not restored until 1947 and then only to a limited audience affluent enough to buy television receivers) reading what was termed 'light' material was more widespread as a leisure activity than it is today.

The social image of crime was, therefore, often as unreal and remote as it was stereotypical. The gangster, often cast in the role of tragic hero, was not always wholly bad. It took the work of the Ealing Studios and their seminal production of *The Blue Lamp* in which PC Dixon, played by Jack Warner,[12] was stationed at Dock Green Police Station, to present an image of crime in a new dimension of social realism.[13]

Part of the stereotypical image derived from the coverage of crime by the press. In 1945 there were many more newspapers than there are today. London had no fewer than three evening papers, celebrated in the newsboys' monosyllabic cry of 'Starnewsastandard!', and every small town supported at least one and sometimes two weekly papers. The reporting of crime, and in particular that of criminal trials, was the very staff of life for popular journalism. Two factors contributed to its success. One was that there were no restrictions on the reporting of court proceedings other than on photography.[14] This meant that, given the protracted nature of committal proceedings in Magistrates Courts in which all the evidence had to be rehearsed and tested by cross-examination before the justices could certify that there was a *prima facie* case to go before a jury, the press had the opportunity of using much of the testimony as news material. Summary proceedings would, in the ordinary course of events, be given some prominence, but matters that had to go to a jury would attract greater attention on account of the kind of prison sentences such offenders would be likely to receive. The other factor was that capital punishment was still the only penalty for murder, and from these proceedings the press wrung every last advantage. In 1945 and for almost the next 20 years every homicide, whether *cause célèbre* or tragically commonplace domestic killing, was newsworthy on account of the potential fate of the accused. The prurient interest of the popular press was often matched by a public curiosity that led to long queues forming outside Assize Courts of those hoping to get into court to catch a glimpse of the prisoner in the dock.[15]

Comparison of pre- and post-war crime

The last complete year of peace was 1938. Although the war did not begin until 3 September 1939, the last quarter of that year was characterized by sufficient disruption to distort the crime figures for that year. From table 3.1 it can be clearly seen that the total of all crime rose by just under 70 per cent in six years from 1938 to 1945.[16] A distinction has to be made, however, between the magnitude of the increase and that of the absolute numbers involved. In 1938, just over a quarter of a million offences had been reported to the police; by 1945, the figure was just under half a million. Examining the figures for particular crimes, the greatest increase took place with respect to property crimes which were in themselves the most common offences. The incentives to commit property crime in 1945 were still considerable on account of the fact that shortages of goods of all kinds were still acute. This goes some way to explain the truly staggering rise in the receiving of stolen property which had almost quadrupled. In 1945 six years of war and the institutionalization of the black market had dulled the moral sensibilities of many people who would be disinclined to 'ask questions' about the source of goods they wanted, albeit somewhat second-hand. Since the bulk of property crime is of a rational economic character, the increase in the serious crime of breaking and entering, which in these data includes criminal entry into both private dwellings and commercial premises, would be explained by the attraction of marginal[17] offenders who would otherwise have remained inactive as burglars.

The rise in sexual offences and other violence against the person was also a matter for concern, although in number they were far fewer than the serious crimes against property. The category of sexual offences includes the gravest of sexual offences, rape, as well as comparatively trivial instances of what the courts held to be indecent assault as well as the crime of indecent exposure, which the law regards as being peculiar to

Table 3.1 Indictable offences known to the police, 1938 and 1945

	1938	1945	Variation (%)
Larceny	199,951	323,310	+62
Breaking and entering	49,184	108,266	+120
Receiving	3,433	10,132	+195
Frauds and false pretences	16,097	13,122	−18
Sexual offences	5,018	8,546	+70
Violence against the person	2,721	4,743	+74
Other offences	6,816	10,275	+51
All offences	283,220	478,349	+69

Source: *Criminal Statistics England and Wales* (London, HMSO, 1952, Cmd 8941)

men.[18] The figures are certainly an underestimate but the increase in reported sexual crime is some indication of the extent to which both sexual constraint and sexual expectations had undergone a profound change during the war years. As far as violence against the person is concerned, it is not easy to find a readily plausible explanation. At the time it was sometimes argued that men, having been trained to be aggressive in war, were now behaving more aggressively as a matter of course. There is little evidence to support this as a general proposition for although there were undoubtedly clinical instances of men having been seriously psychologically disturbed by their wartime experiences by no means all of them turned to crime.[19] While a few of them might have done so, the overwhelming majority of servicemen were well able to discriminate in their responses to friend and foe.

One feature of violent crime is its frequent association with alcohol, and in particular the excessive consumption of alcohol. Men and women in stressful situations often resort to alcohol, and the war years were no exception. But it would be necessary to go behind the raw data to explore just how many of these violent crimes were associated with drink. In drink, people can become provocative and sometimes recklessly so; by the same token, alcohol has the capacity to act as a de-inhibitor of constraint such that aggression – including the response to provocation – may more readily take a violent physical form. Many of these crimes of violence would have been the kinds of assaults and woundings that even today are a common occurrence inside and in the vicinity of public houses, especially those which attract the more marginal elements of a local community. Domestic violence against wives and children, on the other hand, would have been grossly under-represented in these data, partly because the victims themselves seldom complained and partly because when they did the police immediately categorized such violence as a 'domestic' matter from which they sought to withdraw as far as possible.

The only category of offence that registered a decrease between 1938 and 1945 was fraud and false pretences. At just under 20 per cent, this could not be regarded as a very great variation and the lowest figure recorded for the period relates to 1940. The most plausible explanation would seem to lie in the fact that the commission of the offence had been made rather more difficult since the whole population had been registered in 1938–9 and issued with identity cards bearing a number which came to be needed for other purposes. Police officers challenging a suspect would ask for his or her identity card. It was impossible to make a withdrawal from the Post Office Savings Bank[20] without producing the card, and a lost ration book could not normally be replaced save on production of an identity card. Even after 1948 identity numbers were used as a form of identification for purposes of National Insurance.[21] If the civilian population was carefully listed for the first time in history, military personnel were even more closely scrutinized. A man claiming to be a serviceman or to hold a particular rank would immediately have to cite not only his service number but also that of his military unit, all information that could be readily checked by telephone notwithstanding that the computer was still a thing of the future.[22]

What, then, can be said of the state of crime in immediate post-war Britain? Certainly, it had increased since the period immediately before the war and some of the increases, notably in property crime, had been substantial. Nor is it possible wholly to ignore the rise in sexual offences and crimes of violence against the person. On the other hand, the scale of the crime problem was still within manageable bounds. But increasingly after 1945, and particularly as hostility and disenchantment with the Attlee administration grew, popular sentiment was often prone to suggesting that the increased provision of welfare resulted in some sapping of the moral fibre of the nation. Bearing in mind that this was still a time in which such judgements could touch upon a collective nerve, it was but a short step to including increased criminality, and especially juvenile criminality, as one of the perhaps unintended but nevertheless inevitable consequences of the profound social changes that were beginning to unfold.

Against this background the position of the criminal justice system in 1945 is thrown into relief. The police had to cope with a society which was still in almost all its essentials (save the black-out and the large numbers of troops which had prepared for the invasion of Europe) organized on a wartime basis. Police manpower was still affected by these considerations. The prison service, meanwhile, remained in its wartime state, with the borstal system awaiting reconstruction and the whole service reduced in effectiveness. It is one of the ironies of history that the prison service, which approached the task of post-war reconstruction with enthusiasm and a constructive philosophy, achieving a substantial measure of success, is now probably at the lowest ebb of its collective morale and less effective than at any time since the early nineteenth century, while the development of the police service has been almost its mirror image. From unpromising beginnings in 1945, and through a long period of inertia during which corruption scandals were far from infrequent, it has emerged in a modern form aware both of the new technology and its implications for managerial efficiency and the sensitive place that policing occupies in what are now volatile areas of political and social life.

Notes

1 E. Nesbit, *The Railway Children* (London, 1906). It is still in print.
2 In the course of research in the early 1950s I encountered an informant who, on being told of the conviction of a young man

for assault, readily volunteered the information that his father had served eight years for manslaughter some 20 years previously.

3 See *Report of the Commissioners of Prisons for 1955* (London, HMSO, 1956, Cmd 10).

4 Attempted suicide, which remained an offence until 1961, and unlawful carnal knowledge of a female between 14 and 16 years, where the alleged offender was under 17, were instances where the file would sometimes be marked 'no action'.

5 The small number of women stipendiaries did not alter the pattern. I can recall a case in a London court about 1948 in which a first offender was sentenced to three months imprisonment for stealing a bar of soap from his employers, no doubt *pour encourager les autres* (see p. 49).

6 The character of Mr Muddlecombe, a JP created by the comedian Rob Wilton, portrayed the kindly but simple-minded variant of the species. Through the medium of the wireless, Mr Muddlecombe became the comic stereotype of the JP rather as Captain Mainwaring was later to become the comparable comic representation of the Home Guard officer in *Dad's Army*.

7 At the committal proceedings in the Rattenbury murder case in 1935, the Mayor of Bournemouth took the chair and sat with an Alderman and five other justices. See David Napley, *Murder at the Villa Madeira* (London, Weidenfeld and Nicolson, 1988).

8 James Fitzjames Stephen, *A History of the Common Law* (London, 1883).

9 This was done to discourage 'frivolous' appeals.

10 After 1948, when the Criminal Justice Act abolished the power of the courts to order flogging and birching, the attempt of Wing Commander Bullus, the Conservative member for Wembley (1950–74), to have it restored had considerable support among Labour voters if not Labour MPs.

11 The green-covered Penguin books at 6d each (2½ pence in modern money) were extremely popular.

12 Jack Warner had established a national reputation early in the war in the BBC's Saturday night version of the music hall, a variety show entitled *Garrison Theatre*. His catch phrase 'Mind my bike' entered the language of wartime Britain.

13 Dock Green was in real life Paddington Green police station. The television series *Dixon of Dock Green* which followed the film created a folk image of the 'beat bobby' towards which modern policemen are often somewhat ambivalent. In *The Blue Lamp* Dixon was killed in heroic circumstances by a small-time and essentially despicable young villain played by the youthful Dirk Bogarde.

14 Restrictions on the reporting of committal proceedings in Magistrates Courts were first introduced by the Criminal Justice Act 1967.

15 For many years, until the divorce law was reformed in 1971, casual observers would frequent the Royal Courts of Justice in the Strand in the hope of finding a particularly salacious case in progress. Court attendants were not unknown to take tips for directing them towards the 'juicy' cases.

16 Owing to the way in which the statistics were originally presented the crime of robbery, involving theft accompanied by violence to the person or the threat of it, is included among 'other' offences principally because the numbers were small. In 1938 only 127 persons were convicted of robbery and by 1950 the number had only risen to 550.

17 The term 'marginal' is used here in its strictly classical economic sense of those offenders, hitherto deterred from crime because risk outweighed reward, who had found that increased reward now exceeded risk.

18 Under the Vagrancy Act of 1824 a man who 'wilfully, lewdly and indecently exposed his person to the annoyance of passengers' was guilty of an offence.

19 Experiences in the United States with veterans of the Vietnam War are comparable.

20 The Post Office Savings Bank was used on a vast scale by people of moderate means: the expansion of personal banking with the so-called 'High Street' clearing banks is a phenomenon of the late 1960s.

21 Identity cards were not finally abolished until February 1952 by the Conservative administration under Churchill.

22 There is a case, if an arguable one, for some kind of national registration today as a means of limiting some forms of crime and in detecting others. The problem is that of estimating such benefits in terms of the cost to civil liberties.

4 Judges and Magistrates, 1945–1960

Magistrates Courts

The criminal courts in Britain are of extremely ancient origin.[1] Magistrates Courts deal with the bulk of criminal cases; about 80 per cent of all criminal proceedings begin and end in them. In London, the Magistrates Courts, known until the Act of 1952 as 'Police Courts' and often attached to police stations,[2] were in this period staffed wholly by stipendiaries. Lay Justices of the Peace had lost their jurisdiction in the Metropolitan area in 1871 and, save for licensing public houses and off-licences, dealing with juvenile offenders and 'certifying' the mentally ill, did not recover it until 1965. But, in the country at large, unpaid and untrained JPs did the bulk of the work. The office dates from an Act of 1361 passed in the reign of Edward III. The medieval justice combined the roles of policeman and petty judge, as an 'officer of the King's Peace' but, like so many political institutions born of a spirit of pragmatism in time of necessity, the job specification was flexible. Always selected from the ranks of the gentry, by Elizabethan times the JPs were not only responsible for summary justice but for a great many other administrative tasks such as the regulation of wages, indentures for apprentices, fixing the price of bread and administering parish relief to the poor. By the seventeenth century they had become responsible for many of the local gaols and for the houses of correction to which vagrants or 'sturdy beggars' might be committed. By the nineteenth century many of these administrative functions had been transferred into the hands of specialist bodies, or abolished altogether, but as late as 1959 the justices were still responsible for signing certificates of insanity enabling the mentally ill to be committed to mental institutions against their will. They were also responsible for overseeing the management of local prisons until the Courts Act of 1971, and could – and did – in the period after the war order prisoners to be flogged, birched or put on a diet of bread and water. The appointment of JPs left much to be desired and was to be severely criticized by the Royal Commission on Justices of the Peace which reported in 1948.[3]

The problem of the Magistrates Courts was, as far as their sentencing practices were concerned, one in which their essential amateurishness was compounded by their remoteness from any significant sources of intellectual or academic stimulation about the work. Not only were there no training courses for JPs; it was not thought necessary that there should be any. The important exception to this was the bench of juvenile court magistrates in London. Their position was in a sense anomalous in that they were appointed directly by the Lord Chancellor and their names came to him through sources that were substantially less overtly political than those relating to ordinary JPs. They were the only justices in the Metropolitan area who had any criminal jurisdiction and they sat, exclusively, in the juvenile courts. Although there were a number of stipendiaries who specialized in juvenile work, the London juvenile bench was dominated by lay appointments. Perhaps because the juvenile court had a clearly defined welfare role in addition to its criminal jurisdiction,[4] dealing with children and young persons who were 'in need of care, protection and control' but who might have committed no offence as well as with those who had, the appointment of women was one of their distinguishing marks.

While in the rest of the country juvenile work was part of the work of any JP who chose to do it – and many who did were totally unsuited to the task – in London the selection process had resulted in the recruitment of a number of outstandingly capable women, albeit often of very superior social status and not infrequently titled.[5] For many years after the war, until the arrangements were modified, requiring them to gain preliminary experience in the adult court, the London juvenile bench tended to think of itself as a kind of *crème de la crème*, standing in relation to the ordinary magistracy in terms of status rather as officers of a distinguished cavalry regiment might consider their counterparts in the infantry or the catering corps.

It is difficult to assess the influence of this group of juvenile magistrates on their fellows in the adult court. In London they had little influence on the stipendiaries, excepting those who sat in the juvenile court, and ordinary JPs had no criminal jurisdiction. Even after 1965, juvenile justices eschewed much contact with the general body of the magistracy, even those who might be expected to have similar interests through their work in the matrimonial jurisdiction.[6] Outside London they tended to have little influence, save perhaps in the larger centres of population where there was more opportunity for public meetings and the interchange of ideas.

A small number of magistrates were members of the Howard League or the Institute for the Study and Treatment of Delinquency.[7] Meetings and residential conferences at which a number of professionals in the criminal justice system often made a generous input were an important medium of such interchange. The Prison Commissioners in particular frequently used meetings of the Howard League as a public platform for the promulgation of their policies. The notable absentees were the senior members of the judiciary.

Legal education

It was not until the Institute of Criminology at Cambridge was founded in 1960 that academic criminology acquired sufficient respectability for any of Her Majesty's judges to take seriously the notion that there might be other considerations in the management of crime and the sentencing of offenders other than those immediately presented by the nature of parliamentary statutes or the past practices of other judges. Even then, they did not congregate in large numbers and the higher judiciary is still today probably sceptical, if somewhat less hostile, towards the proposition that there can be a legitimate arena of intellectual discourse on these matters outside the closed worlds of the courts and the judges' lodgings.

No small part of the problem arises from the nature of legal education, and in this context a comparison might be drawn between its inadequacies and the nature of higher education in the nineteenth century. Beneath the surface of legal education, certainly in the early years of this century when those who were in high judicial office in the late 1940s and 1950s were acquiring their education, it is possible to identify a number of principles. One is that law is essentially the subject of a highly privatized system of knowledge, its very language serving as a device to exclude outsiders from sharing it. Another is that precedents are to be given respect, even though they might arise from very specific and personal interpretations of the law by particular judges. Yet another is that there is but a single set of moral precepts upon which judgments may be made and a common morality binding upon all citizens, notwithstanding that they might look remarkably like those cherished by the 'respectable' middle classes from whose upper echelons lawyers were recruited.

In a curious sense, too, legal education in England was, and still remains, anti-intellectual in that it expects students to acquire knowledge, normally by rote, rather than to examine propositions in terms of their utility or moral propriety. The profession of the law tends, therefore, to be tardy in moving with the times and slow to absorb knowledge and ideas that derive from other disciplines. In the nineteenth century higher education had a decidedly unscientific bias, and only after the demands of manufacturing industry became insistent did science and technology acquire a status equal to that of history or classics.

The law at this period had still not taken on board anything of significance from either psychology or psychiatry. Criminals were assumed to be rational creatures who intended the consequences of their acts and, moreover, thought consciously and deliberately about them in advance. The distinction between psychology and psychiatry was often imperfectly understood and the forensic psychiatrist was generally thought to be a person who sought somehow to *excuse* the behaviour of the criminal by giving an explanation for it that might seem to defy the authoritative wisdom of common sense as well as rejecting conventionl morality. A medical witness who perhaps sought to explain an offence of shoplifting in terms of the accused's menopausal disturbance would receive short shrift, but such defences were rare.

It was in the capital cases that the defects of legal education were to be seen most clearly. In 1843 the judges had been asked to determine some guidelines on the subject of insanity as a defence following the assassination attempt on Sir Robert Peel by Daniel M'Naghten who, because he did not know what Peel looked like, had killed his secretary, William Drummond instead. M'Naghten was found to be insane; he had paranoid delusions about Peel and was to become one of the first inmates of Broadmoor in 1863. The M'Naghten Rules, as they came to be known, were paraphrased by the great Victorian psychiatrist Henry Maudsley as having two parts: (i) either the accused did not know the nature and quality of the act, or (ii) if he did know it, did not know it to be wrong.

The Rules, which have been described as having both the flexibility of a Procrustean bed and the rigidity of an army bunk,[8] depending upon the judge who is interpreting them, bore little indication of familiarity with how the human mind works. Very few offenders do not know the difference between squeezing a child's neck and squeezing an orange[9] and even fewer do not know that killing people is widely held to be wrong as well as against the law.[10] By concentrating upon cognition rather than the pathologies of behavioural motivation, the rules were largely useless save in the very few cases where the offender was so utterly deranged as not to know who or where he was.[11] Medical thinking about the nature of 'madness' had changed a good deal since 1843, but in the late 1940s and 1950s legal thinking had changed not at all. Indeed, it was hostile to new concepts such as 'personality disorder' and 'psychopathic personality'. There were those in practice and on the Bench who had known, during the First World War, of deserters and men who refused to go back to the trenches being court martialled and shot for cowardice, men whom we can now almost certainly say were battle casualties as surely as if they had lost their limbs. But the idea of an offender – military or civil – being able to advance such a defence seemed contrary to all sense and propriety; offenders were not 'sick' but 'wicked' and it was maintained that one could not confuse the two.[12] Forensic psychiatrists were not, on the whole, eager to go into the witness box and when they did they frequently had a very unpleasant time under cross-examination.[13]

One of the consequences of this state of affairs was that a number of murderers, almost certainly seriously mentally disordered, were hanged. Probably the most notorious case after the war was that of Neville Heath. Heath conformed to the classic description of the aggressive sexual psychopath. He was also a convincing impostor, posing as an Air Force officer although he had in fact been court martialled and dismissed from the South African service. In 1946 he returned to England and, in the course of a series of violent sexual episodes, brutally murdered two young women, savagely mutilating them in the process. Evidence as to his mental state was given by W. H. de B. Hubert[14] but, as was to be the case in the Haigh trial three years later, the absurd format of the M'Naghten Rules made it a child's play for the prosecutor[15] to make the witness appear extremely foolish.[16] Neither Heath nor Haigh could be in any sense described as other than extremely unpleasant specimens of humanity, but the enormity of their crimes was itself indicative of their abnormality, if nothing else. The 'monster' image was one which was projected by the press, in some cases for all it was worth. In the Haigh case the defendant had made a statement in which he claimed to have drunk the blood of his victims; this story reached Fleet Street and the editor of the *Daily Mirror* decided to publish a somewhat lurid account of the vampire-like activity and the disposal of the bodies in acid, but without actually mentioning the accused's name. For his pains, the editor, Sylvester Bolam was arraigned for contempt of court before the Lord Chief Justice, Lord Goddard, and sentenced to three months' imprisonment. The paper was fined £10,000 and ordered to pay costs, an enormous sum in 1949.

Lord Chief Justice Goddard

No account of the period of the late 1940s and 1950s could exclude reference to the dominance in the criminal courts of

Rayner Goddard. From his appointment in 1946 until his retirement in 1958, he was an *éminence grise* who overshadowed the whole process of criminal justice. Born in 1877 and educated at Marlborough and Oxford while Queen Victoria was still on the throne, he became Recorder of Poole in 1917 and went on from there to Recorderships in Bath and Plymouth until, in 1932, he was elevated to the King's Bench Division. In 1932 he became a Lord Justice of Appeal. At the end of the Second World War Goddard was not only one of the most senior judges but certainly one of the most experienced in criminal matters if only because he had been dealing with crime in a judicial capacity for almost 30 years. He was also 69 years old. Compared with Travers Humphreys; who was ten years his senior, he was not by any means the oldest judge on the High Court Bench. The principal difficulty arose from the fact that, having practised at the Bar before the First World War, when there were still judges about who had been colleagues of men like Fitzjames Stephen, his views about crime and punishment were set in time; a time that was long since past. He was 40 when he first attained judicial office and 55 by the time he reached the High Court. During the 1930s he had had the experience – some would say the misfortune – of serving under Gordon Hewart of whom it has been written: '[he] stands well placed to be one of the least satisfactory of the Lords Chief Justice of England – rude, arrogant, disputatious and with little of the milk of human kindness.'[17]

Many of those who appeared before Goddard would consider that he shared some of these unenviable qualities. On the Bench he presented a fearsome and positively cadaverous appearance; he did not disguise the fact that he had no sympathy for criminals and certainly none for those who sought to mitigate their crimes by providing social or psychological explanations. He was contemptuous of psychiatrists, social workers and probation officers and made little secret of the fact that he approved of corporal punishment and hanging.[18] The case for which he is probably best remembered is that involving Derek Bentley in 1953.

Bentley, aged 19, had gone with another youth, Christopher Craig, to a wholesale confectionery warehouse in Croydon one night in December 1952; it is presumed with the intention of breaking in and stealing. The youths were surprised by police and Craig, who was 16, was said to have discharged a revolver after Bentley (who was by this time being physically held by the police) is alleged to have shouted 'Let him have it, Chris!' A shot rang out and one of the officers who was attempting to arrest Craig was killed.[19] Both were convicted of murder but Craig, who was two years under the minimum age for the death penalty, could only be sentenced to be detained at Her Majesty's Pleasure. Bentley, as an accessory, was sentenced to be hanged.

It was then – and still is – a rare event for a policeman to be gunned down in cold blood and almost unknown for the assailant to be a 16-year-old boy. But as the trial proceeded the popular view inclined to the idea that it was Craig who had been the ringleader and Bentley the one who had been led along. Whatever the truth, the failure of Bentley's appeal and the fact that it seemed a gross miscarriage of justice that the one who had been convicted of firing the bullet would escape with his life while the other, who all along had maintained that his words were intended to mean 'Let him have the *gun*', was to die.

After the appeal was dismissed, but before execution was carried out, the Home Secretary, Sir David Maxwell-Fyfe reviewed the case as was customary in all instances where the death sentence had been passed to consider whether it would be appropriate to recommend the exercise of the Royal Prerogative of Mercy to commute Bentley's sentence to one of life imprisonment. In the course of his deliberations he consulted Goddard. It is not known what advice Goddard gave and, although it has since been suggested that he *expected* that Maxwell-Fyfe would recommend a reprieve, the fact remains that he did not and Bentley was hanged at Wandsworth Prison.[20] The execution occasioned a degree of public outrage that was not to be matched until the hanging of Ruth Ellis in July 1955 and one consequence of it was the wide reinforcement of the belief that Goddard had advised that the hanging should go ahead.

Goddard was 76 at the time of the Craig and Bentley case and it did nothing to enhance his reputation, although it must be said that both the nature of the law of murder and the mandatory character of the only two sentences available – death for those of 18 and detention at Her Majesty's Pleasure for those of lesser years – gave a judge no latitude for manoeuvre once the jury had reached a verdict. But that was not how things were seen by the more liberal-minded sections of public opinion. Only if Goddard had urged a reprieve on Maxwell-Fyfe and his urging had acquired the status of an open secret would it have done anything to change an image that was becoming fast fixed in the popular consciousness: that of an irascible, reactionary old man who was rapidly becoming an enthusiastic misanthropist.

He continued as Lord Chief Justice until he decided to retire from the Bench in 1958. This was not before the Homicide Act of 1957 had come into operation – under which Bentley could not have been hanged – and one of Goddard's last cases in the Court of Criminal Appeal was that involving Albert Matheson, a mentally retarded psychopath of 52 who had killed and dismembered the body of a 15-year-old boy who had been his homosexual partner. He had then taken a registered envelope from the boy's clothing containing £35.

Quite unusually in such cases, there was no dispute as to the accused's low IQ (73) or his psychopathic personality. The medical officer of Durham Prison took the view that he was a psychopath with a mental age of ten years. Under the 1957 Act, murder in the course of theft was capital, but Matheson's plea was one of diminished responsibility, for which the Act provided the penalty of manslaughter and the court of Criminal Appeal, consisting of Goddard and four other judges, ruled that the jury's verdict had been unreasonable and against the weight of the evidence substituting a verdict of manslaughter under S. 2 and imposing a sentence of 20 years' imprisonment. It was a sound and clearly reasoned judgment, but Goddard clearly could not resist a sting in the tail. He could understand that in this case, 'a crime of the most horrible description, so revolting as to be almost beyond belief', that the jury might think that 'such a monster ought not to live and therefore only a capital sentence was appropriate' but they, their Lordships, had to bear in mind the present law.[21] Goddard was by now 81.

Intellectually, Goddard's performance was wholly undiminished; what was so evident by 1958 was that he was, by reason of temperament as much as by age itself, becoming increasingly a man wholly out of his time, inflexibly unable to accommodate either new thinking in the world of criminal justice or changes in public opinion which was increasingly articulate as well as critical of the traditional attitudes of judges. (Perhaps he himself secretly recognized that he was no longer fitted for judicial office.) He lived on until the age of 94 and, although in 1971 he had been off the Bench and out of the headlines for more than a decade, the various bland obituaries were nevertheless accompanied by more astringent recollections of his performance.

Goddard was not alone as a gerontocratic incumbent of judicial office, and if there were a large number of judges and stipendiary magistrates, to say nothing of JPs, who were sitting well into their seventies, it is as much a commentary upon the structure of the legal profession and the systems of appointment to judicial office as upon any assumed belief in the superior wisdom of the middle-aged and elderly. Sybil Campbell, the first woman stipendiary, was 33 when she was called to the Bar in 1922 and 56 when appointed to Tower Bridge Magistrates Court in 1945, after having been in the wartime Civil Service. She retired in 1961 at the age of 72 and displayed similar qualities of longevity, eventually reaching the age of 88. Campbell was as feared among the petty malefactors of Southwark and Rotherhithe as was Goddard among the more professional villains who frequented the Old Bailey. Like him, she became something of a legend in her lifetime and remains unforgotten nearly 30 years later.[22]

The 1960s: catalyst of change

The decade of accelerating change in British society was to be that of the 1960s. There are some who regard it as a decade of positive change and liberal progress; others perceive it as the beginning of a moral decline in British society, the time in which seeds were sown that are now being reaped in the form of increasing crime, vandalism and social incivilities.

To some extent, those are value judgements coloured by the political inclinations of the viewer. What cannot be disputed is the fact that it was a reforming decade in which legal and judicial reforms made up a substantial part. The law relating to suicide and male homosexuality was liberalized. The censorship of plays and books was relaxed and at the end of the decade the death penalty for murder was abolished.[23] In 1965 the system of appointing JPs was to be radically overhauled and in future they would be obliged to undergo at least elementary training. Meanwhile, there were to be stirrings in the legal profession, both about the nature of legal education and the possibility of improving the sentencing practices of the higher courts. Whatever their shortcomings, the courts of the 1980s are very different from those of 40 years ago and operate very different penal policies in a climate that has become, paradoxically, *more* rather than less critical.

Notes

1 The references in this context are essentially to England and Wales. Arrangements in Scotland, although similar with respect to police and prisons, differ importantly in the courts. This is because the law in Scotland is based on Roman law which differs in its essential principles from the English common law (whose writ was extended in past centuries to both the conquered Welsh and the Irish). The situation in the Province of Northern Ireland is further complicated by the fact that the Six Counties had a measure of home rule from 1921 until 1972, have always had an armed police force and are the subject of certain criminal legislation specific to the Province.
2 Bow Street is a notable example.
3 *Report of the Royal Commission on Justices of the Peace* (London, HMSO, 1948, Cmd 7463).
4 The first juvenile courts were officially established in 1908 after a successful experiment begun in Birmingham in 1905. The Children and Young Persons Act 1933 both confirmed their dual role and enhanced their status. Women had always played a predominant role in the field of juvenile welfare. See Anthony Platt, *The Child Savers: The Invention of Delinquency* (Chicago, University of Chicago Press, 1969).

5 The names of Professor Barbara (later Baroness) Wootton and Dame Eileen Younghusband are noteworthy in this connection.

6 In the large new London court buildings in which both adult and juvenile courts sit, often on a daily basis, juvenile magistrates only very rarely sit at the lunch table with other magistrates and even then, tend to sit apart in the practice of some self-imposed ordinance against commensality. This is in complete contrast to the 'Mess' principle which is part of the institutional framework of the Inns of Court, is replicated by the Bar 'on circuit' and is a feature of both the Crown and Magistrates Courts.

7 The Howard League for Penal Reform was formed in 1921 by the amalgamation of the Howard Association and the Penal Reform League. The ISTD had been founded in the 1930s and was closely associated with the work of the Portman Clinic where various forms of psychotherapy, owing much to Freudian theories, were available for the treatment of children with behavioural problems.

8 Sheldon Glueck, *Law and Psychiatry* (London, Tavistock, 1962).

9 But the question was put in precisely this form at the (second) trial of John Thomas Straffen in 1952.

10 Lord Chief Justice Goddard had ruled that 'did not know it to be wrong' could only be interpreted as 'did not know it to be against the law', see R. V. Windle [1952] 2 QB 826.

11 The number of people before the courts who are totally 'unfit to plead' on account of their being able neither to understand nor participate in the proceedings is extremely small.

12 It is, of course, perfectly possible to view an action as 'wicked' or 'bad' while at the same time recognizing the actor to be the victim of a mental disorder.

13 For example, Professor Henry Yellowlees, a most distinguished figure in his field, at the trial of John Haigh the so-called 'acid bath' murderer in 1949. This was a celebrated trial. The prosecutor was the Attorney General, Sir Hartley Shawcross, while Sir David Maxwell-Fyfe, later to become Home Secretary in the Churchill administration and eventually Lord Chancellor (as Lord Kilmuir) led for the defence. The trial judge was Sir Travers Humphreys, then in his 83rd year who, as Professor Keith Simpson observes in his *Forty Years of Murder* (London, Harrap, 1978), was known for his 'inhospitality to any psychiatrist who ventured to appear as an expert witness in his court'. Humphreys, who had been born in 1868, was called to the Bar in 1889 and appeared at the trials of Oscar Wilde, Crippen, Seddon, Smith (of the 'Brides in the Bath'), Sir Roger Casement, Bottomley and

Thompson and Bywaters. The *Dictionary of National Biography* records that 'The story of Humphreys' life is the story of the criminal law of his time.' He had been a Treasury counsel and became Senior at the Old Bailey in 1916. The *DNB* also notes that it was once said of him in this role: 'He's so damned fair that he leaves nothing for the defence to say.' For an account of Humphrey's conduct of the Rattenbury trial in 1935 see David Napley, *Murder at the Villa Madeira* (London, Weidenfeld and Nicolson, 1988), which provides a superb picture of the conduct of a major criminal trial in the interwar period. It gives a somewhat different impression of the man from that of Simpson.

14 It was Hubert, together with Sir Norwood East, whose report in 1939 established the need for a psychiatric prison which eventually opened in the early 1960s. There are no fewer than five books about Heath, and several others in which he's a major subject. The most recent and among the most interesting is Francis Selwyn, *Rotten to the Core: the life and death of Neville Heath* (London and New York, Routledge, 1988).

15 In this case Sir Anthony Hawke, QC, later to become Common Sergeant at the Old Bailey.

16 Keith Simpson in his autobiography, *Forty Years of Murder*, is rather less than fair to this pioneering figure in forensic psychiatry when he refers to his part in the case.

17 See David Napley, *Murder at the Villa Madeira*, p. 203.

18 He recommended on more than one occasion from the Bench that parents should not hesitate to beat their children as soundly as the circumstances required.

19 The Craig and Bentley case raised – and still raises – important questions for both criminal jurisprudence and forensic criminology. Quite apart from whether Bentley should have been convicted, let alone hanged, doubts have even been raised about the veracity of the prosecution evidence about who fired the fatal shot. Some of these issues are discussed in H. Montgomery Hyde (ed.), *The Trial of Christopher Craig and Derek William Bentley* (London, 1954), which deals with legal aspects of the case, and in a review of the book by J. E. Hall Williams in the *British Journal of Delinquency*, 6 (1954) no. 2. An account of local reactions to the national press coverage are to be found in Terence Morris, *The Criminal Area* (London, Routledge and Kegan Paul, 1958). Probably not since the young George Stoner had been under sentence of death for his part in the Rattenbury affair in 1935 had there been such a groundswell of public sentiment for the condemned man.

20 Craig was released in 1963 on the advice of the then Home Secretary Henry Brooke (later Lord Brooke of Cumnor). The information had been leaked to the press in advance and the matter was raised in the House by Col. Marcus Lipton, the Labour member for Brixton.

21 For the report of Matheson's appeal see [1958] WLR 474. Also Terence Morris and Louis Blom-Cooper, *A Calendar of Murder* (London, Michael Joseph, 1964).

22 See also chapter 3, note 5.

23 Though *not* capital punishment, which remains the penalty for treason and setting fire to Her Majesty's dockyards and arsenals. It is possible that under an unrepealed statute of Henry VIII adultery with the consort of either the sovereign or the heir to the throne remains a capital offence.

5 Policing, 1945–1960

Modern British policing has its origins in Sir Robert Peel's 'New Police' who were introduced to London in 1829. The Metropolitan Police, as they became known, are the forerunners of all the modern police forces in England and Wales and in Scotland. While Secretary in Ireland, Peel had laid the foundations of the Irish Constabulary some years before. In England, he had been able to draw on a tradition in London established by Henry Fielding in the middle of the eighteenth century with his Bow Street Runners and Patrick Colquhoun with his river police towards the end of the century.

Initially, there was great hostility to the New Police, born of a not altogether unfounded anxiety given the ruthless deployment of the 'new' Napoleonic police in France by Fouché. Given, too, that Peterloo and the Six Acts had been events of but ten years before, fears that the New Police would be as interested in the surveillance of political radicals as they would be in making the streets of London safer places were understandable.

In the event, the founders of the Metropolitan Police were very much concerned with the latter objective and only much later with the former. The growth of London and the incompetence of the ancient system of parish constables (the 'parish' system in London was itself breaking down) was such that the need for a competent constabulary was urgent. The service that emerged from the efforts of Charles Rowan, a distinguished and forward-looking ex-soldier who had served with Wellington at Waterloo, and Richard Mayne, a lawyer who was to prove to be an outstanding administrator, set new standards in the maintenance of social order. Every effort was made to ensure that the new constables were competent, well disciplined and resistant to corruption.[1]

The object of policing was to be the prevention of crime and the ensuring of public tranquillity, and in this context it was determined from the outset that the New Police should carry no firearms, being equipped with nothing more than a stout truncheon.[2] One consequence of this was to set a 'threshold of force' which was both socially acceptable and less likely to result in mortal injuries. By the mid-1860s every county and borough in the country had a police force that had been modelled upon the 'Met'.[3] But this is not to say that the social acceptance of the New Police or its regional counterparts was universal; in the cramped city slums of London and Liverpool, Birmingham and Glasgow, officers normally had to patrol in pairs and there were districts that were to all intents and purposes 'no-go' areas.[4] In the more affluent suburbs in which an emerging lower middle class was beginning to enjoy an increased prosperity, the police were, in contrast, seen as the defenders and guarantors of tranquillity, which included protection from street crime and burglary.

By the 1930s it could be argued that there were two distinctly different images of the police. Those at the lower end of the social scale saw them as essentially hostile. It was the police who arrested and brought before the magistrates those who were tramping the roads in search of work and who slept 'rough' unable to give a good account of themselves. It was the police who arrested the street bookmakers,[5] and the men who sat about on doorsteps playing cards or 'pitch and toss' for small sums of money and the police who rounded up women in the 'red light' districts who were plying their trade as street prostitutes.

For the respectable working class who shared many values with the middle classes the perception was altogether different. The police were the largely deferential custodians of the peace whose role it was to assist and befriend the citizen who needed help and advice. A policeman could tell you the time, direct you to an unknown street and, if you were a child, see you across a busy road. In a powerfully symbolic way, the tall man in blue, tunic buttoned to the collar and with headgear redolent of the military fashions of Queen Victoria's day, represented a tangible manifestation of security. It was a special sort of security that foreigners could never hope to enjoy. Those foreigners were often said to remark that they found British policemen 'wonderful'.

The avuncular image of the police was not always entirely serious. W. S. Gilbert had parodied the New Police in *The Pirates of Penzance* and, in children's literature both Ernest the Policeman in Hulme-Beaman's classic of BBC Children's Hour *Toytown* in the 1930s and 1940s and Mr Plod in the later stories of Enid Blyton made the policeman into a figure of fun – slow-witted almost to the point of being bovine. The positive side of the avuncular image reached its apotheosis, however, in the figure of Dixon of Dock Green.[6] This positive quality was a reflection of the notion that the ordinary police officer was, in effect, no more than a 'citizen in uniform'. This idea was clearly articulated by the Royal Commission on Police Powers and Procedure in 1929 which included in its report the following profoundly important proposition:

> The police of this country have never been recognised, either by law or tradition, as a force distinct from the general body of citizens. Despite the imposition of many extraneous duties on the police by legislation and administrative action, the principle remains that a policeman, in the view of the common law, is only 'a person paid to perform, as a matter of duty, acts which if he were so minded he might have done voluntarily'.[7]

Whether this was true in 1929 is a matter of opinion; whether it could have been held to be true in 1945 is more doubtful. As a thesis today it is demonstrably untenable since the nature of policing has become immensely technical and the powers of the police *qua* police officers immeasurably greater than those possessed by ordinary citizens. What is important about the proposition – and the fact that it is still cherished as an ideal stereotype – is that it is related to an image of policing that is essentially 'user friendly'.

Police training

During the period of the war police manpower had been

maintained by the use of a War Reserve including pensioners who had returned to service and Specials who were employed on both a full- and part-time basis. In 1944, when thoughts of post-war reconstruction were very much in the air, the government had set up a committee comprised of representatives of the Home Office and Chief Constables to consider both the short-term requirements of the first years of peace and a long-term strategy. First among its concerns was the training of the police.[8]

Throughout the 1930s, and indeed before, this had been a very patchy affair, with considerable variation between the 183 separate forces in England and Wales.[9] In the Metropolitan force Trenchard, who had been the founding father of the Royal Air Force in 1919 and appointed Commissioner for the Metropolis by the MacDonald government in 1930, had ideas for training that did not become popular in the police service. The Metropolitan Police College at Hendon only lasted from 1934 until the outbreak of war in 1939 but a negative recollection of it is deeply embedded in the folk memory of the Police Federation. It was to be, in essence, a source of 'officer' material with two routes of entry, one from the force by competitive examination or, exceptionally, by special recommendation and the second directly from the universities by means of examination or academic qualification. Not surprisingly, ordinary beat officers, the majority of whom would have left school at 14, took the view that they stood little chance of getting to Hendon; rather, they saw their chances of internal promotion diminishing in consequence of the graduate entry.[10] Nothing, of course, had changed as far as the appointment of Chief Constables was concerned; they were still to be recruited from the ranks of retired military personnel.

The idea of a national police college had been considered in 1929, but there were numerous objections to it, not least from those who saw it as the thin end of the wedge in the creation of a national police force. Trenchard had resigned in 1935 and his successor, Air Vice Marshal Sir Philip Game was not to prove as faithful to his blueprint for training. By 1938 Game concluded that the Hendon scheme needed to be drastically revised, and accordingly direct entry was limited to six applicants a year and all had to serve for a year as a uniformed constable before being admitted. In the event, the new arrangements were never implemented and at the outbreak of war Trenchard's Hendon was closed.

Two themes, 'nationalization' and 'rationalization' can be discerned in the thinking surrounding the plans for reconstruction. Clearly, there were too many separate police forces for there to be either any development in efficiency or any benefits of economies of scale. But by this time the municipal character of the institution of policing had become deeply entrenched by nearly a century of tradition. Fears about the political consequences of a centralized police force under the control of the government were largely on the left of the political spectrum,[11] and by 1945 Labour was in power with a steam-roller majority. But one of the characteristics of the thinking behind 'nationalization' – public ownership is perhaps a more accurate term – was that in the area of public utilities rationalization and the benefit of economies of scale would improve efficiency. Major rationalization was not to occur on a significant scale until the Police Act of 1964,[12] but a small beginning was made in 1948 with the establishment of the National Police College at Ryton-on-Dunsmore in Warwickshire.

It was the first tangible product of the Joint Committee of 1944 and open to the whole establishment of serving police officers. The idea of an 'officer class' identified with socially superior outsiders and which had been anathema to the Police Federation was finally given decent burial. From humble beginnings, the college grew in both sophistication and academic standing, and removed in 1960 to a magnificently preserved Jacobean house at Bramshill in Hampshire, a striking contrast to the wartime industrial hostel in which it had begun. Bramshill has succeeded in opening up opportunities for young constables that would have been beyond the dreams of those in service in 1945. It has facilitated the promotion of young men in their twenties to the rank of sergeant and inspector and perhaps, even more important, provided a springboard for them to enter the universities for first degree courses in a wide range of subjects.[13]

The Metropolitan Police

Just as Peel's New Police dominated the development of modern policing throughout the country, so the Metropolitan Police has tended to dominate policing in the present century.[14] At the end of 1944 Herbert Morrison who was by this time Home Secretary in Churchill's War Cabinet had the task of finding a successor for Air Vice Marshal Game. The man he invited was neither a retired army officer nor an Air Marshal but a career civil servant, Sir Harold Scott, who was at the time Permanent Secretary at the Ministry of Aircraft Production.[15] By the standards of the time it was a most unusual appointment and with only three exceptions (including Sir Richard Mayne, the founding co-Commissioner) the 'Met' had always been commanded by a retired military officer of high rank. As is often the case when only the decisions and not the reasons behind them are recorded, it is uncertain why Morrison should have taken this unusual step. Scott himself suggests that Morrison wanted to emphasize the civilian character of policing.[16] David Ascoli, on the other hand thinks that a more plausible explanation might lie in the nature of the politics of succession in the Home Office itself.[17]

The problems involved in the policing of London immediately after the war were complicated by various factors. For reasons that are far from clear, the increase in serious (indictable) offences during the period 1938–46 had been of the order of 34 per cent, little more than half the national increase. We have no certain way of knowing whether this difference was genuine or spurious. It could have been that given the special characteristics of the capital city, fewer offences were reported in London than in the rest of the country. But, as Scott recorded in his first annual report as Commissioner for the year 1946 (he had taken over from Game in June 1945) London had its special problems. Even an increase in crime of a third was still a major problem, not least because the strength of the 'Met' was lower than at any time since the mid-1880s. London's streets were once again filled with traffic since the restoration of the civilian petrol ration brought large numbers of cars that had spent the war locked up in garages back on to the road.[18]

Not least of the problems affecting London and directly connected with the shortage of recruits was the shortage of police housing. Trenchard had been responsible for a building programme that provided for accommodation in Section

Houses, akin to the quarters provided by the Prison Commissioners for their staff. This programme had been halted by the war and in 1945 all the attention of the government was on the provision of housing for the civilian population at large. A housing allowance for police officers was far from being a complete solution to the problem since the shortage of housing affordable to police officers, when even in 1948 the weekly pay of a constable was still only £5.25, was acute. The police during the period 1939–45 had seen a situation which exactly paralleled that of 1914–18, a virtual stagnation in wage levels compared with those of industrial workers who during wartime were not only able to bargain for substantial wage increases but also had the benefit of virtually unlimited overtime.

The unsatisfactory state of police pay and the housing shortage deterred recruitment, although the Police Act of 1946 had provided for a modest increase which had raised a constable's pay to the sum just quoted.[19] What was even more acute a problem was the loss of some 2,700 officers whose retirement had been 'frozen' during the war, many of whom were by now well beyond normal pensionable age. What the Metropolitan Police lacked in manpower was to some extent compensated in technological advantages. Trenchard had invested in police cars, many of them equipped with wireless linked to a central information room at New Scotland Yard. In 1937, with the cooperation of General Post Office, the '999' emergency telephone system was inaugurated. Meanwhile, in 1935 the 'Met' became the only force in the country to have its own forensic science laboratory. A mounted division had been established in 1919, and in 1946, under Scott, six Labrador retriever dogs had been introduced into the suburban divisions for detective work.

Police manpower

Throughout the period of the first Labour administration police manpower, both in London and the provinces, constituted a serious limitation to police effectiveness. These were the years of full employment and a time when wage rates in industry, geared to expansion and the export trade, put the public services at a distinct disadvantage, the police not excluded. Early in 1948 it became clear to Chuter Ede, the Home Secretary, that the shortage of police in London was indicative of a national problem. He established a committee under Lord Oaksey to examine the conditions of service for the police in the whole United Kingdom. Given extremely broad terms of reference, the committee addressed itself to both the quantum of police pay and the nature of the negotiating machinery for future settlements. The result was that a year later it recommended that the starting pay of a constable should be raised to £330 per annum (at this point police pay began to be expressed in annual rather than weekly terms) which was an increase of £1.10 per week; rising to £8.08 after 22 years' service. Pay for sergeants was raised to £445 per year or £8.56 per week. To accommodate the special problems of living in the capital, a 'London allowance' of £10 per year was instituted, later doubled to £20.

The British police have had an unenviable experience in their attempts to gain the right to belong to a trade union. Immediately after the First World War a joint police and prison warders' union was savagely crushed,[20] and union membership was to all intents and purposes regarded as a disciplinary offence – and certainly a not infrequent cause of dismissal – in both services until the war. The Oaksey Committee put forward the idea of a non-statutory Police Council for Great Britain with an official side and a staff side representing all ranks, presided over by an independent chairman, with provision for referring disputes to a panel of three arbitrators chosen by the Prime Minister. This arrangement was made statutory by the Police Act of 1964.[21] The effect of the Oaksey award was disappointing; not until the significant improvement in police pay of the 1970s was police strength to come up to establishment. Some forces, however, went ahead with the innovation of recruiting police cadets, boys aged 16–18 years who, in the years before their National Service, were employed on general duties in police stations.

There was also a somewhat guarded programme of recruitment of women officers. The position of women in the police has always been somewhat anomalous in the sense of being the subject of prejudice among male police officers at every level. It has partly to do with the nature of policing which in its 'action' mode has always presented an essentially masculine image and only very recently have women officers been able to establish their parity with male colleagues.[22]

Public attitudes to the police

In 1945 it could be confidently said that, with the probable exception of those sections of society who because they lived by or in the shadow of crime had no reason to respect the police,[23] the overwhelming majority of ordinary people held the police service in high regard and were consequently minded to place their sympathies with them when complaints were made about police behaviour. By the mid-1950s this picture began to change. Hitherto police corruption had been a matter largely kept from public view and probably concentrated within the detective branch of the Metropolitan service. But in 1956 the Chief Constable of Cardiganshire became the subject of disciplinary proceedings arising from allegations of incompetence in the administration of the force. The net effect of these proceedings was the amalgamation of the Cardiganshire force with that of neighbouring Carmarthenshire. The following year a rather more sinister event occurred involving allegations of corruption against three officers of the Brighton Borough Police, one of whom was no less a person than the Chief Constable. At their trial, the two junior officers were convicted and sentenced to imprisonment while the Chief Constable was acquitted, but this was not to be the end of his troubles. The Watch Committee promptly dismissed him with the consequence that he forfeited his pension.[24] He pursued what he, and the House of Lords was eventually to hold, was a breach of the rules of natural justice by the committee in the course of the dismissal proceedings and his pension rights were reinstated.

1957 was to prove a bad year for the police, for no sooner was the Brighton affair out of the headlines than two other events took its place. One involved the trial, conviction and imprisonment of the Chief Constable of Worcester for fraud, the other allegations of assault on the part of two constables in Scotland on a juvenile who had given them insolence. This was the youth who was to acquire a brief but incandescent place in public consciousness as the 'Thurso Boy'. By this time the political atmosphere was sufficiently charged for R. A. Butler, who had become Home Secretary in the new Macmillan administration, to set up an investigation under the 1921 Tribunals of Inquiry (Evidence) Act.[25] The conclusion of the tribunal was that the boy had been the subject of a minor assault following his provocative conduct but that had the matter been prosecuted under Scots law it was in their view unlikely that a conviction would have followed on the evidence that was before them.[26]

While the Thurso case was under the scrutiny of the tribunal trouble struck again, this time in the 'Met'. The well-known comic actor, Brian Rix[27] was stopped whilst driving across Putney Heath by one PC Eastmond who alleged that Rix was speeding. A Mr Garratt, a civil servant, who had been driving behind Eastmond pulled up and became involved in the interchange between Rix and Eastmond. An altercation ensued, during which it was alleged that one of the participants was thrown into a hedge. Garratt was arrested and taken to the local police station where Eastmond sought to charge him with assault on a police officer. The inspector on duty, however, formed a different judgement of the situation, refused to accept the charge and in consequence Garratt was released. He, not unnaturally, was not a little aggrieved and commenced a civil action against Eastmond for assault and battery and against the Commissioner of the Metropolitan Police for false imprisonment.[28] As has often been the case, the matter never came to court and Garratt accepted £300 in compensation out of police funds 'without prejudice', i.e. without any admission of liability. No disciplinary action was taken against Eastmond.

What might have been no more than a trivial incident once more, like the Thurso case and possibly because of it, became the focus of parliamentary attention. The issue in Parliament addressed the general question of police powers and police accountability. What was important was that neither Rix nor Garratt could be dismissed as members of the criminal classes who would naturally concoct mendacious allegations against the police. Even if the payment to Garratt had been *ex gratia*, there must have been some perception of fault on the part of the police and, if so, why had Eastmond not been subject to disciplinary proceedings? Why, given the nature of the *prima facie* evidence, had the station Inspector declined to accept the original charge? Was it true that Eastmond had been transferred from traffic duties on account of other, as yet publicly unventilated, complaints by other members of the public against him? All these questions were, in one way or another, expressed in public and specifically parliamentary debate. The idea was abroad that there was a potential conflict between police powers and civil liberty, and the constitutional implications were almost self-evident.

But before the appointment of the Royal Commission on the Police under the chairmanship of Sir Henry Willink, QC, in January 1960,[29] yet another incident occurred which must have confirmed Butler's thoughts about the necessity of a thorough-going inquiry into the constitutional position of the police. In July 1959 a dispute between the Chief Constable of the City of Nottingham and his Watch Committee resulted in the suspension of the Chief Constable. Captain Athelstan Popkess was a policeman of forthright opinions who had earlier achieved some national notice by being the first Chief Officer of Police to institute a policy of prosecuting motorists for obstructing the highway as they 'kerb-crawled' in search of professional prostitutes. This dispute involved members of the local authority, and Popkess, having consulted the Director of Public Prosecutions, had conducted an investigation into the claiming of expenses and the cost of some work carried out by the council. The Town Clerk and the Watch Committee had asked him to supply them with details of his investigation, which he refused to do. The dispute had been going on for some time, and this refusal resulted in his suspension by the Watch Committee. Popkess took the view that the request was an unwarranted interference in the process of criminal justice and quite improper; the Town Clerk, on the other hand, took the view that the police inquiries had been biased. The Home Secretary, to whom Popkess appealed, considered that for him to have acceded to their request would have been a breach of his duty. The Watch Committee accordingly reinstated the Chief Constable who, however, decided to retire at the end of the year.

The Popkess case was, perhaps, an extreme example, but it nevertheless illustrated some of the problems that had developed in the three-way relationship between the police, the police authorities and the Home Office. Clearly, there were constitutional issues affecting police powers and the relationship between Chief Officers of Police and their police authorities.[30] But in the public mind it was probably the question of police accountability that was uppermost. The ancient question *quis custodiet ipsos custodes?* (who shall keep an eye on the keepers?) was seen as important, not least because by now there were too many instances of both allegations and proved instances of police impropriety and corruption for the idea that 'our policemen are wonderful' not to be subject to qualification.

The Royal Commission on the Police

The Royal Commission reported in two parts. The first appeared in November 1960 and was concerned with police pay, which had again fallen behind levels in industrial occupations which competed for manpower from the same sector of the labour market. Since the Oaksey award in 1948 the pay scale for constables had been increased to £510 per year, rising to £695 after nine years' service; Willink recommended a scale of £600 to £910 with supplements of £30 after 17 and 22 years. The London allowance remained at £20. What the Royal Commission also recommended was a triennial review of pay in relation to wage rates in some 18 other industrial occupations. Since this was a time of public concern about increasing crime, and police manpower was seen as the primary means of controlling its growth, improved pay was justified in terms of the need to recruit more policemen for the purpose. What was not perhaps fully appreciated was that an increasing proportion of police time was being spent on duties other than the prevention, detection and prosecution of crime. As society became more affluent, car ownership increased by leaps and bounds with the consequence of growing problems of traffic management that were becoming especially acute in the central London area. London, too, had a major problem of street prostitution which probably reached its height in the mid-1950s.

The most important part of the Royal Commission's work

was to appear in May 1962. Its deliberations on the constitutional issues were lengthy and fundamental.[31] It supported the traditional view that the authority of a police officer is 'original, not delegated and exercised at his own discretion by virtue of his office'.[32] It considered suggestions that the time was now ripe for a national police force under central control but, with the exception of the dissenting voice of Dr A. L. Goodhart,[33] came down in favour of the existing structure of local arrangements. Goodhart's argument was a powerful one and he came close to persuading the rest of the Commissioners to his point of view – that central control actually provided more not fewer democratic safeguards against impropriety.

It is to the Willink Commission that we owe the beginnings of the modern system of complaints investigation. This consisted of allowing Chief Constables to invite senior officers from other forces 'independently' to inquire into complaints. It recommended the appointment of a Chief Inspector of Constabulary who would report to the Home Secretary, and also suggested that the Home Secretary should have greatly increased powers over provincial forces, making the Home Office the dominant partner in the existing tripartite structure. The Commission also felt that there were still too many separate police forces and that further amalgamations should be vigorously pursued. The majority of the Commission's recommendations were incorporated in the Police Act of 1964. It was an important year – and not only for the police. For in October the Labour Party won the general election with a majority of four seats. It was the end of 13 unbroken years of Conservative government and was to mark, in political terms, the end of the 'post-war period' and the beginning of the new age of the 'white heat of technology'.[34]

Notes

1 In the early days a major problem was drunkenness on duty. In 1863 no fewer than three sergeants and 212 constables were dismissed for this reason. See David Ascoli, *The Queen's Peace* (London, Hamish Hamilton, 1979).

2 Firearms in 1829 were in any event clumsy to operate, unreliable

in their effects and could be a danger to their users. The modern revolver, the successor to the pistol beloved of highwaymen, did not appear until Colonel Sam Colt patented his famous weapon in the US in 1835.

3 Rowan and Mayne, the first two (joint) Commissioners actually produced their outline plan for the organization of the force in a mere 12 weeks.

4 For example, in London, the Old Jago in Hoxton which was to be the first major demolition project of the London County Council. For an account of life in such areas see Arthur Morrison, *A Child of the Jago* (London, 1896; reprinted London, Penguin Books, 1946); and Raphael Samuel, *East End Underworld: The Life and Times of Arthur Harding* (London, Routledge and Kegan Paul, 1981). At the time of Raphael's research, Harding was probably the last person alive to have been brought up in the Jago.

5 Off-course betting, except with a bookmaker over the telephone, was illegal until the reform of the gambling laws in 1968. For references to 'sleeping rough' see Hermann Mannheim, *Social Aspects of Crime in England between the Wars* (London, Allen and Unwin, 1940).

6 See chapter 3, note 14.

7 Royal Commission on Police Powers and Procedure, *Report* (London, HMSO, 1929, Cmd 3297).

8 The first report was *Higher Training for the Police Service in England and Wales* (London, HMSO, 1947, Cmd 7070).

9 The three smallest, the Liberty of Peterborough, Tiverton Borough in Devon and that of Clitheroe in Lancashire, had establishments of 10, 11 and 15 respectively.

10 But, as David Ascoli notes, there were 20 'insiders' and only 12 'outsiders' on the first course in 1934. On the second the numbers were 20 and 8 respectively, see Ascoli, *The Queen's Peace*, p. 234.

11 They resurfaced during the miners' strike of 1984–5 when the National Reporting Centre, operated under the auspices of the Association of Chief Police Officers (ACPO) on the premises of New Scotland Yard, gave a convincing impression that a national police force might only be round the next political corner.

12 The Act laid a general responsibility on the Home Secretary for securing the effectiveness and efficiency of policing arrangements in the country as a whole, not unlike his responsibilities for London, saving the fact that in London the Home Secretary *is* the Police Authority. The number of forces in England and Wales is now only 43. See also note 19 below.

13 Not only are there a substantial number of graduate police officers,

a growing number pursue specialist criminological studies to MPhil and PhD level. Bramshill is administered and financed by the Home Office with a board of governors representative of the police service and local authorities.

14 About 25 per cent of current Chief Constables – and an unknown number of other senior officers – either began their careers or at some time served in the 'Met'.

15 David Ascoli records that Morrison is said to have asked him 'Can you ride a horse?' Ascoli, *The Queen's Peace*, p. 255.

16 Harold Scott, *Scotland Yard* (London, André Deutsch, 1954).

17 Ascoli, *The Queen's Peace*, p. 255.

18 In 1946 a modest petrol ration was restored to civilian users other than those with 'essential' needs, and 'pleasure motoring' was once more possible. The ration was finally abolished in 1951 although it was briefly – and ineffectually – rationed during the Suez Crisis in 1956. One consequence of the return of traffic to the roads, apart from traffic problems, was an increase in offences relating to motor vehicles. Another was the growth of dishonest activity centred on the second-hand car trade.

19 The Act provided for the reduction of the number of police forces in England and Wales. By 1948 the 183 existing forces had been reduced to 131. By 1960 the number was down to 125. Finally, after the Police Act 1964, the number has settled at 43.

20 See C. W. Reynolds and Anthony Judge, *The Night the Police went on Strike* (London, Weidenfeld and Nicolson, 1968). Trenchard, in 1934, was still totally hostile to unionization.

21 The model was clearly the Civil Service system of 'Whitley' councils. Neither the Police Council, nor the Whitley council relating to the prison service has ever been popular either with the Police Federation (the union for policemen below the rank of superintendent) or the Prison Officers' Association.

22 The current situation is still far from equitable. In the Royal Ulster Constabulary it was recently felt impossible to deploy women officers in a paramilitary situation, and it is still not always easy for a woman to be posted to a mounted branch. The image of women officers in an essentially *affective* role, caring for children and women and consoling the bereaved, is very persistent. The police service has long had a very masculine image of itself, and in the post-war period anti-feminism was entrenched. See Allison Morris, 'Women as criminal justice professionals', in her *Women, Crime and Criminal Justice* (Oxford, Basil Blackwell, 1987).

23 Bearing in mind that some of these crimes, like street book-making, were to disappear as a consequence of legislation.

24 At that time borough police forces were overseen by committees of the local authority that took their name from the ancient concept of 'watch and ward' dating back to the Statute of Winchester in 1285.

25 The use of such a power is rare and in this instance was highly unpopular with the police. Compare the objections of the Metropolitan Police Commissioner, Sir David MacNee to the establishment of the Scarman Inquiry into the Brixton riots in 1981 under S.32 of the Police Act 1964. His argument was that it made the focus of the inquiry the conduct of the police. The 'Met' found it very difficult to accept the idea that its actions could have precipitated the disorders.

26 *The Allegation of Assault on John Waters* (London, HMSO, 1959, Cmnd. 718).

27 Now Sir Brian Rix, Director of the charity MENCAP. At the time he was a well-known national figure, highly regarded for his brilliant farces at the Whitehall Theatre.

28 The Commissioner of the Metropolitan Police was at this time Sir Joseph Simpson. Having joined in 1931, he had pursued a brilliant police career, becoming the first Metropolitan Commissioner to have risen from the rank of constable.

29 David Ascoli seems to have allowed his personal perception to colour his explanation of Butler's decision to set up the Royal Commission and speaks of 'Once more, a Home Secretary [finding] himself with the pack baying at his heels' (Ascoli, *The Queen's Peace*, p. 275). Butler had announced the setting up of the Commission in the course of the censure debate (613 HC Deb. cols 1239–1303), hardly the kind of thing upon which so experienced a minister would suddenly seize in the flush of the debate. The parliamentary concern was seriously expressed and Butler's reaction far from being a case of 'bowing before the storm' was a characteristically statesmanlike response to a legitimately voiced constitutional anxiety.

30 It seems inconceivable that the Popkess case could not have been in the forefront of Butler's mind in his decision to set up the Willink Commission. The Eastmond case, which had occurred in December 1958, by itself, at most justified no more than a Tribunal of Inquiry on the lines of the Thurso affair.

31 For an excellent account of the Royal Commission of 1962, see Ian Oliver, *Police, Government and Accountability* (London, Macmillan, 1987).

32 Simmonds, LJ, *Attorney General for New South Wales* v. *Perpetual Trustee Co Ltd* [1955. AC 477].

33 A. L. Goodhart, *Memorandum of Dissent* (London, HMSO, 1962, Cmnd 1728).

34 A memorable phrase employed by Harold Wilson in addressing the Labour Party Conference at Scarborough in October 1963.

6 Progress and Reform, 1945–1960

In 1945 courts, prisons and the police service were still encapsulated in their pre-war organizational structures and, perhaps more importantly, in their pre-war organizational thinking. In the 15 years following the end of the war, six under Labour administrations and nine under Conservative, the pressures on all three elements of the criminal justice system were unrelenting. Crime, which had increased by some 70 per cent during the war years, did not settle to an even level but continued to increase. Of the three, the effect upon the courts was the least evident for magisterial justice was generally summary, sometimes being swift to the point of farce.[1] Pressures on the police, though considerable, were seldom publicly visible. The position with regard to prisons was altogether different.

Penal reform

From 1877 the prison system in England and Wales had been administered by the Prison Commission. Before that date, long-term convict prisons had been the responsibility of the Home Office, and local gaols had been under the control of local magistrates. A consequence of this arrangement was that while the Home Office was able to establish a standard regime for convict prisoners and a moderately competent system of management, the local gaols presented a chaotic picture, ranging from the highly innovative and constructive to the totally mismanaged. While some institutions were characterized by a modicum of humanity, others were the source of criticism and scandal.

The Act of 1877 that centralized the entire prison system was, in principle, a step in a sensible direction but the outcome was not altogether a success. The principal reason for this was to be found in the personality of the first Chairman of the Commissioners, Sir Edmund du Cane. Like many of the great public servants of his time he had, before becoming an Inspector of Prisons, been an army officer. His views on crime and punishment were simple and severe; his conception of administration totally autocratic. Until his retirement three days after the publication of the report of the Gladstone Committee in 1895, which was a damning indictment of his regime, he ruled the prison system with a rod of iron and became increasingly pitiless towards inmates and subordinate staff alike. By the end of his regime, life for the English convict had much in common with that of the inmates of Dostoevsky's *House of the Dead*. Du Cane was succeeded by his deputy, Sir Evelyn Ruggles-Brise who was responsible for introducing a new system for dealing with young offenders that took its name from the local gaol at Borstal, near Rochester, where it began. His career was not altogether memorable.

Although middle-class offenders[2] had made an occasional appearance in prison from time to time, the situation changed in the years immediately before the outbreak of war in 1914 when the Women's Social and Political Union, led by Mrs Pankhurst, pursued a vigorous public campaign in support of women's right to vote. Many of the women demonstrators were arrested and imprisoned in the course of which some went on hunger strike and were forcibly fed.[3] These women, who were almost always of superior social status to the wardresses who had charge of them, brought to the attention of a wider public the conditions under which ordinary prisoners, often incarcerated for petty offences or unable to pay fines, were forced to subsist. Awareness of conditions in male prisons was increased when during the war numbers of conscientious objectors were also imprisoned. By 1919, the penal reform movement had been given a considerable fillip. Stephen Hobhouse and Fenner Brockway, with the encouragement of Beatrice and Sydney Webb, began a major private investigation of the prison system under the auspices of the Labour party[4] and its results were published in 1922 under the title *English Prisons Today*.[5] Ruggles-Brise, who had retired a year earlier, was succeeded by Sir Maurice Waller, but the dominant influence on the Commission throughout the inter-war period was to be Sir Alexander Paterson.

Waller and Paterson began rapidly to make the changes that Hobhouse and Brockway's charges had rendered imperative. They did not ameliorate prison conditions overnight; indeed, it could be argued that there were relics of the Edwardian prison system still in evidence in 1945, but a process of 'humanization' had undoubtedly begun.[6] What was fundamental to the approach that Paterson successfully engineered was an insistence on the primacy of rehabilitation as an ideal and an objective as distinct from the deterrent and punitive philosophy of du Cane, the effects of which had not been eradicated during the Ruggles-Brise regime.

Second only to their commitment to the rehabilitative ideal was their concern to influence public opinion. To this end they made no secret of their contacts with the Howard League and the redoubtable Margery Fry.[7] Throughout the inter-war period the predominant thrust of prison administration was reformist, the individual Commissioners making frequent public speeches describing their innovations and often using the Howard League and its publications as a platform. The Prison Commissioners were to continue in this vein until the Commission was abolished and its work subsumed into that of the Prison Department of the Home Office in 1964.

Two matters particularly exercised their attention: the problem of young offenders and that of persistent offenders. The system of 'preventive detention'[8] introduced by the Act of 1908 was, by 1930, seen to be virtually ineffective in dealing with the stage army of persistent offenders, many of whom committed only trivial offences, and in 1932 a Departmental Committee that had been set up a year earlier reported on the subject.[9] The Committee had distinguished between those who were habitual and those who were merely on the road to becoming so and accordingly proposed different arrangements for the two categories.

As the 1930s progressed, so the emphasis on imprisonment

diminished in favour of non-custodial alternatives of which probation orders were the most popular. But penal reformers were considering other, more imaginative, measures for dealing with offenders, especially the younger variety. By 1938 a variety of proposals had become sufficiently firm to be incorporated into the Criminal Justice Bill of 1938. As a consequence of the gathering political crisis, the proposed legislation was still-born and it was left to the Attlee administration of 1945–50 to begin again.

Penal reform did not immediately press upon the government's attention, but by November 1947 there was a Bill before Parliament. What it sought to do differed very little from the intentions of the 1938 proposals. It addressed the question of persistent offenders and proposed a system of preventive detention based upon the seriousness of the offence – as indicated by the potential penalty – and the number of times the offender had been similarly convicted in the past, with a minimum sentence of five years and a maximum of 14. For those of less developed criminal habits, it introduced what was to become known as 'corrective training' for which the offender had similarly to qualify, in this case for a sentence of not less than two and not more than four years. Corrective training had a particularly unpopular feature that rankled with many who received it; instead of being able to earn one-third remission for good behaviour, the corrective trainee could be released on licence but was subject to recall during this period to serve the remainder of his sentence if he misbehaved.

The Bill also provided for 'detention centres'. These were to be residential institutions in which the regimes would be brisk and the sentence brief in order to provide a deterrent for young offenders between the ages of 12 and 21, shorter than either borstal or approved school but, by being custodial, more rigorous than probation. In the light of new knowledge about the psychological component in some criminal offences, it was proposed to make it possible for courts to order a period of residential treatment in a mental hospital or attendance at an outpatient clinic for a period not exceeding 12 months as a condition attaching to the probation order.

Yet another innovation was the 'attendance centre' arising out of a suggestion of the Howard League that had been incorporated in the 1938 Bill. In its earlier form it was intended to be available for offenders of all ages, but in 1948 the suggestion was limited to young offenders who would have to give up a proportion of their free time on Saturdays to attend at centres where they would be required to participate in a variety of activities, not necessarily of their choosing.

In these essentials, the Bill became law as the Criminal Justice Act 1948. It had all the characteristics of the motor cars that were being produced at this time for export to the rest of the world. For just as the Austins, Morrises, Wolseleys, MGs and Humbers that were coming off the assembly lines were all based on pre-war designs dusted down for re-use,[10] so too all these proposals for penal reform had been developed and articulated in a pre-war world. It had taken no less than 16 years for the recommendations of the Committee on Persistent Offenders to get on the statute book. The question of whether these measures were appropriate to a changed and changing post-war world seemed not to be raised, in contrast to so much of the constructive thinking that had gone on in other fields of government activity. There had been nothing to correspond to the work of the Home Office committee on the police that had been set up in 1944.[11]

It would be an exaggeration to say that the Act made an impact upon the problem of rising crime. As far as the provisions for persistent offenders were concerned, the courts still managed to send petty offenders to preventive detention because they qualified on the grounds of having been convicted of offences for which imprisonment of two years or more *could* be imposed; the fact that it need not actually have been imposed upon them in the past was neither here nor there.[12] Preventive detention prisoners were entitled to only one-sixth as distinct from the normal one-third remission for good behaviour, and after 1948 disputes arose in prison because those men still serving sentences under the 1908 Act had privileges, like strips of carpet in their cells, that were not available to the 1948 men. As far as corrective training was concerned, the courts at first used it with some enthusiasm which however waned as the figures for reconvictions suggested that neither the sentence nor the regime constituted any specially potent formula for dealing with the problem of what to do with young men apparently bent upon a lifetime of crime. As the corrective trainee numbers fell, they had to be accommodated in prisons that had been designated for training purposes, where they found themselves alongside other young men serving sentences of similar length but of simple imprisonment; it was hardly surprising that their unfavourable position regarding licence, as distinct from remission, was a source of friction.

Only very small numbers of women were sentenced to preventive detention and corrective training during the time that these sentences were on the statute book.[13] Most were middle-aged and elderly women who had pursued a generally unprofitable career of petty theft and fraud; they were nuisances rather than dangers to society but that did not prevent them from being held in a special part of Durham Prison during this period.

By the mid-1950s it had become clear that neither of these two sentences was other than counter-productive as far as the management of prisons was concerned and they fell into a long period of desuetude before finally disappearing in 1967.[14]

The Commissioners did not seem at all enthusiastic about implementing the novel system of detention centres. It had been widely suggested at the time that the idea of a 'short sharp shock', to use the phrase that entered the popular imagination, was a *quid pro quo* to those sections of the higher judiciary and the magistracy who regretted the fact that the 1948 Act had deprived the courts – but not the prison Boards of Visitors – of the power to order flogging and birching.[15] The Report of the Commisioners of Prisons for 1955 records no fewer than ten instances of prisoners who were flogged with the cat-of-nine-tails in the year ending 31 December 1954, receiving between them 124 lashes, two of them no fewer than 18 lashes each. By comparison, the solitary prisoner who received six strokes of the birch seems to have got away lightly.[16] It was the visiting magistrates and Boards of Visitors who dealt out these punishments; the prison authorities had merely to administer them. The Commisioners in their public utterances made no secret of their distaste for corporal punishment and the slowness with which they proceeded towards the idea of the detention centre suggested a similar distaste. For whatever reason, *festina lente* appeared to be their motto and the first junior centre for boys aged 12–16 years did not open until 1952. A second opened in 1957 and meanwhile a third had been provided for the 16–21 year age group. There was no provision for girls until 1962.

There is little doubt that as the rehabilitative ideal was in the ascendant it would have been a positively schizophrenic exercise for the Commisioners to seek to devise a regime that was bleakly deterrent; as a matter of course thought went into the construction of training programmes which included among other things education classes and attempts to deal with illiteracy. As time passed, it became increasingly difficult to distinguish the specific character of detention centres from the regime in borstals; only the brevity of the sentence effectively told them apart.

The attendance centres developed on an altogether more haphazard basis, being only available in a few urban areas. Again, the nature of the regime was problematic as far as those charged with the running of them were concerned.[17] At some centres boys had to get down on their hands and knees to scrub floors or do physical training, while at others they had classes in motor mechanics, the making of model aeroplanes and talks about civics.

The Criminal Justice Act of 1948, though it was thought at the time to be a major piece of legislation, proved to be little more than a penological dinosaur, obsolete in its conceptions and largely unadaptable to the changing world of post-war Britain. It did nothing to alleviate the difficulties of a prison system that was effectively reforming itself through the direction of its enthusiastic Commissioners; those were the problems that stemmed from the increased size of the prison population which could be checked only by legislation that limited the powers of the courts to imprison. These were to come in the 1960s, limiting the imprisonment of young offenders under 21 and first offenders in whose cases courts had to certify in the register their reasons for passing such a sentence.

Abolition of the death penalty: the issue that would not go away

It is an ironic twist of fate that although the Criminal Justice Act accomplished comparatively little that was of lasting importance, the occasion of the Bill provided a launching pad for what must be the most important theme in post-war penal reform: the abolition of the death penalty. From the standpoint of an observer in 1989 it may be difficult to appreciate the emotions and opinions that surrounded the death penalty when it was part of the law of England. Some of the MPs who have taken part in recent debates about the propriety of its reintroduction were in school when the hangman plied his trade and others in the population at large have no recollection of those times at all.[18] Throughout the post-war period those in favour of abolition had been hard at work. A number of cases, including those of Thompson and Bywaters in 1923 and Rattenbury and Stoner in 1935, had not only excited the popular imagination but had demonstrated some of the inbuilt absurdities of the law affecting murder as it then stood.[19] For although there was always the exceptional instance of brutal and apparently senseless killing, it was the dominance of domestic murder that emphasized its essentially tragic quality. And not least important among the arguments in the abolitionist armoury was the fact that in the crime of murder, deterrence, in the form of the death penalty, was scarcely ever a relevant consideration.

It was almost common knowledge that the 1938 Criminal Justice Bill that had been introduced by Sir Samuel Hoare, later Lord Templewood, would be revived as soon as the war was over and the National Council Against the Death Penalty, a group which worked with the Howard League until final abolition, wrote to Chuter Ede the new Labour Home Secretary in 1946 reminding him that the Labour Conference of 1934 had voted in favour of abolition and that it had been the minority Labour administration of 1929 that had appointed the Select Committee on the Death Penalty that had recommended an experimental period of abolition.

Chuter Ede was something of an unknown quantity on the issue, unlike Templewood who had become President of the Howard League and a publicly proclaimed abolitionist. Ede had voted in 1938 for an experimental five-year period of abolition, but had never been active in the abolitionist lobby. The Parliamentary Penal Reform Group, organized by the League, had arranged for 187 MPs to sign a memorial to the Home Secretary asking him to include in the Criminal Justice

Bill a provision for a five-year period of suspension along the lines recommended by the Select Committee in 1930. This was in July 1947, four months before the publication of the Bill. At the same time, Ede received a joint deputation from the League and the National Council which formed the view that Ede was by no means certain about his position. Churchill, meanwhile, as leader of the opposition had refused even to see a deputation from the National Council accompanied by a small number of Conservative abolitionists.[20] When the Bill was finally published, it contained, to the consternation of the abolitionists, no clause relating to capital punishment.

During the second reading, Ede argued that he was now convinced that capital punishment did deter; he confused the argument by saying that rising crime made it impossible to consider an experimental period of suspension, given that public opinion was in favour of retention. There was, of course, the fear that if the Bill were to include a controversial issue like the death penalty it could be lost in the Lords which at that time could delay Commons matters for two years. There was also a not inconsiderable lobby behind the scenes from the police and from the prison service which were firmly in favour of hanging. These pressures must have been sufficient to convince Herbert Morrison, now the Labour party's chief strategist, that the matter was too hot to handle.[21] While Attlee, an essential constitutionalist, was not a man to use a majority in the Commons to ride roughshod over what he perceived to be the drift of opinion in the country. But there were problems for the political managers. That there were no fewer than 187 signatures to the memorial meant that back-bench opinion could not be discounted, and accordingly it was decided that while ministers would have to vote collectively with the government, back-benchers could have the benefit of a free vote.[22] It was Sydney Silverman on the back-benches who tabled an amendment at the report stage of the Bill to suspend the death penalty for five years. It was agreed by 245 votes to 242. The course of events in the Lords was to be altogether different where there was not only a majority in favour of retention but a vocal presentation of the retentionist position by no less a personage than the Lord Chief Justice, Lord Goddard who in the course of what was a maiden speech, treated the House to a catalogue of grisly forensic detail in support of the case for hanging.[23] The Lords defeated the Silverman amendment by 181 votes to 28. The government was in a quandary; it faced the prospect of the wrath of a majority of its supporters in the Commons if it did nothing, while it faced certain defeat at the hands of the Lords if it persevered with the amended Bill.

A compromise was attempted which in effect proposed that there should be degrees of murder to which the penalties of death and life imprisonment should variously apply. This was approved by the Commons by 307 to 209 but again foundered in the Lords by a vote of 99 to 19. The debates had taken place during the spring and summer, and in the parliamentary recess it became clear to the party managers on the government side that the matter had been at the centre of political interest for too long. The way to put it on to the back burner, given the parliamentary strength of the abolitionists, was to set up a Royal Commission. This was announced in November, the government being careful to set its terms of reference so as to exclude consideration of abolition itself, and to consider only the ways in which liability to suffer the death penalty might be limited or modified, what alternative punishment could be substituted and what changes in the law and the prison system would be involved in any alternative punishment.[24]

The Royal Commission on Capital Punishment 1949–53, whose Chairman was Sir Ernest Gowers and its secretary Francis Graham-Harrison,[25] deliberated upon the topic with immense care, notwithstanding the way in which Chuter Ede had carefully excluded outright abolition from its terms of reference. It finally reported in September 1953.[26] It would have been perverse of the Commission not to have taken the view that the so-called M'Naghten Rules were an unsatisfactory test of mental responsibility. Indeed, whether they were ever satisfactory can be reasonably doubted, but by the 1950s it was impossible to find any figure eminent in the field of psychiatry who considered them other than worse than useless.[27] It was the judges, led by Goddard whose enthusiasm for the gallows seemed to increase rather than diminish, who clung to the idea that they represented a reasonable basis for forensic argument. Cynics took the view that they did so in order to ensure that no one charged with murder should escape the gallows if they could help it.[28] The Gowers Commission came up with a formula not unlike what was eventually incorporated into the Homicide Act of 1957, referring to 'disease of the mind or mental deficiency' of such a degree that the accused ought not to be held responsible. As to the question of establishing degrees or categories of murder the Commission was totally opposed, holding the task to be impossible. Gowers was later to describe the attempt to define categories of murder – as many attracted to compromise in 1948 had attempted to do – as a 'search for the chimera'.[29] Perhaps their most controversial suggestion was that the jury be empowered to decide in each case whether on the evidence the penalty should be death or life imprisonment. Recognizing that the disadvantages of this arrangement might well outweigh the merits they concluded that it

> would seem to be inescapable that in this country a stage has been reached where little more can be done effectively to limit the liability to suffer the death penalty, and that the issue is now whether capital punishment should be retained or abolished.[30]

Although the report was debated in the Lords, the government, now headed by Churchill, provided no time for a debate in the Commons until February 1955, in spite of repeated questions to ministers about the government's intentions regarding it.

Although there was in the country a general feeling in favour of retaining the death penalty, three particular cases involving murder aroused not only an extraordinary degree of public interest, but considerable doubt about the fairness of the law and claims about its infallibility. In the case of Craig and Bentley early in 1953, it was the idea that Bentley should hang while Craig went free that was repugnant to many who were nevertheless in favour of capital punishment.[31] The second case was that of the multiple murderer John Christie of 10 Rillington Place, North Kensington.

Early in 1953 the bodies of six women, including Christie's wife, were found in the house.[32] Unusual though this mass murder was, there was yet another twist to the case for it was in an upstairs flat in this very house in 1949 that Timothy Evans and his wife and baby daughter had lived. Mrs Evans and her daughter had been found strangled in an outside wash-house. Evans, an illiterate man of limited intelligence, gave himself up to the police but made several contradictory statements, some admitting the killings and others in which he claimed that Christie had killed his wife while attempting to abort her. Christie, a former War Reserve policeman, was the principal witness for the Crown and Mrs Christie the second. Evans was convicted of the murder of his baby daughter and sentenced to death. Chuter Ede refused a reprieve and he was hanged on 9 March 1950.

But now, in 1953, Christie admitted not only to the killing of the women whose bodies had been found, but also of Mrs Evans in 1949. He categorically denied, however, having murdered the baby. He entered a plea of 'guilty but insane' at his trial which the jury did not accept and he was sentenced to death on 25 June 1953. The problem was obvious: the similarities between the killings, the methods employed, the places in which the bodies were hidden and the keeping of newspaper cuttings all suggested that if the guilt of Evans had been properly established there had been two murderers living at the same address in 1949, one an illiterate, inarticulate, mentally retarded lorry driver and the other a former police officer who was capable of being an accomplished witness in a murder trial.

Under considerable public and political pressure, the Home Secretary, Maxwell-Fyfe, appointed John Scott-Henderson, QC, to conduct an inquiry into both the Evans and Christie cases. It was to be held in private, and before Christie was hanged. When published it stated that he was of the opinion that Evans had been properly convicted of the murder of his baby daughter; that he had no doubt but that Evans had killed his wife, and that Christie's confession to her murder was both unreliable and untrue.[33] The inquiry had taken Scott-Henderson just one week and Christie was hanged at Pentonville the day after its publication. Maxwell-Fyfe would accept no criticism of the way in which the inquiry had been conducted, but during 1953 there seemed no way of keeping the names of Evans and Christie out of parliamentary or public consciousness. Much later, another inquiry by Mr Justice Brabin was to be conducted very differently and with very different results.[34] But it is significant that by the time the Gowers Report came to be debated in February 1955, Chuter Ede, who had signed Evans's death warrant and refused a reprieve, was prepared to admit that the Evans case showed that a mistake was possible.[35]

The third case, which was to prove to be the most dramatic in that it involved the hanging of a beautiful young woman, was that of Ruth Ellis. A divorcee and mother of two children, she led a life that left much to be desired by the standards of suburban morality, having not one but two lovers at the same time. One of them was a young man of shallow and immature disposition who had ambitions to become a top motor racing driver. She was pregnant by him and Ellis claimed that in an altercation – he apparently wished to sever the liaison – he had struck her repeatedly in the abdomen causing her to miscarry. Three days later she waited for him to come out of a public house in Hampstead and shot him dead. At her trial neither her hysterical state following the miscarriage, nor the evidence about the assault persuaded the judge that the evidence was sufficient to reduce the crime from murder to manslaughter and on 22 June she was sentenced to death.

Not since the Rattenbury trial 20 years before had there been such a *crime passionnel* and in this instance all the sympathy was for Ruth Ellis. In spite of hundreds of letters in the press and a petition to the Home Secretary of over 2,000 names, he decided on 11 July that she must hang. The hanging of Ruth Ellis in Holloway on the morning of 13 July can only be described as a national trauma. *The Times* the next day reported that a crowd of 500 had spent the night in a vigil at the prison gates to be joined in the morning by more than a thousand others, same praying, some weeping, some chanting over and over the names 'Evans! Bentley! Ellis!' For more than a week the newspapers were full of letters and editorial comment, and by this time the interest of the American and European press was focused on the Ellis case producing banner headlines in France, Italy, Germany and the United States.

Major Gwilym Lloyd George who had succeeded Maxwell-Fyfe as Home Secretary had moved in the debate on the Gowers Report that the House do no more than 'take note' of its recommendations. Silverman once more introduced an amendment to suspend capital punishment and in the debate it became clear that Lloyd George, who had been an abolitionist in 1948 was now strongly in favour of the death penalty while Chuter Ede, chastened no doubt by his misgivings at having authorized the execution of Evans, had become an abolitionist. The amendment was lost by 245 votes to 214.

The pressures for reform did not diminish. The indefatigable Silverman attempted a private member's bill with predictable lack of success, but the issue would not go away. The pressure increased in particular for a full-scale debate but the government's dilemma was that one which incorporated a free vote would result in a victory for the abolitionists. Finally, it determined upon a motion in February 1956 that while the death penalty should be retained, the law of murder should be amended.[36] From then on, events moved rapidly. The government motion was defeated by 293 to 262 and an abolitionist amendment passed largely as a consequence of the votes of Conservative abolitionists. The government, now presided over by Eden, agreed to provide facilities for Silverman to introduce an abolition bill which proceeded to pass through all its stages in the Commons only to reach a dead stop in the Lords where it was defeated by 238 votes to 95. Once more the government was forced back to a compromise and, after taking political counsel during the summer recess, introduced its own Homicide Bill in November. This was to become law as the Homicide Act in March 1957.

Macmillan had succeeded Eden as Prime Minister and Butler had become Home Secretary by the time the Bill went to the Lords to be decided not by a free vote but under the whips. Far from throwing it out, their Lordships accepted it with alacrity. Goddard, the Lord Chief Justice and now in his 81st year, was curiously silent on its introduction of degrees of murder, an arrangement he had earlier castigated as unworkable. For what the Homicide Act of 1957 enshrined was the very principle that the Gowers Commission had considered chimerical, and it was not to be long before the absurdities of the categories of capital and non-capital murder were to become evident. What the Act accomplished on the positive side was the effective relegation of the M'Naghten Rules to the museum of legal history. In their place, it provided a definition of 'diminished responsibility' that made sense in terms of modern psychological medicine.[37] It also provided for an extended defence of provocation by words and well as deeds[38] and for a defence of manslaughter to be available to the survivors of suicide pacts.[39] But if it reduced the number of executions, it did little to diminish the anxieties about the possibility of mistakes in capital cases which continued until the death penalty was finally abolished.[40]

Given that at this time the total number of persons indicted and standing trial for murder was between 100 and 150 a year – a tiny proportion of the total of all alleged offenders – it is difficult to appreciate the intensity of feeling that the issue of the death penalty aroused. It demonstrated, perhaps, that in the political process the moral dimension of an issue can command immense interest and involvement far beyond its statistical magnitude.

Notes

1 This was especially true of the London stipendiary courts that sometimes processed up to 70 or 80 drunks and vagrants in a morning. Then, as now, about 80 per cent of all criminal business began and finished in the Magistrates Courts. For accounts of this period see Lionel Fox, *The English Prison and Borstal Systems* (London, Routledge and Kegan Paul, 1952); and Leon Radzinowicz and Roger Hood, *A History of the English Criminal Law*, vol. 5 (London, Stevens, 1986).

2 Oscar Wilde was a notable example.

3 Forcible feeding in British prisons, as a result of which some prisoners choked to death, was discontinued at the time of the IRA prison hunger strikes in the 1970s.

4 Hobhouse was a conscientious objector and nephew to both Professor L. T. Hobhouse and Beatrice Webb. Fenner (later Lord) Brockway was also a conscientious objector and both had been imprisoned for refusing military service. Stephen Hobhouse and Fenner Brockway, *English Prisons Today* (London, Longmans, 1922).

5 The work was done in the teeth of Home Office opposition which included thinly veiled threats of prosecution. It had a major impact on penal reform.

6 See Fox, *The English Prison and Borstal Systems*, pp. 67ff.

7 Enid Huws Jones, *Margery Fry: the Essential Amateur* (London, Oxford University Press, 1966), p. 121.

8 The Prevention of Crime Act 1908 had instituted a 'double track' sentence; one, often comparatively short, for the offence in question and another, much longer, in respect of being a habitual offender.

9 Departmental Committee on Persistent Offenders, *Report* (London, HMSO, 1932, Cmnd 4090).

10 The one notable exception was the Standard Vanguard.

11 See chapter 5, note 8.

12 A prison joke that circulated in the 1950s ran as follows: First convict: 'Is it true you got an eight for nickin' a shirt?' Second convict: 'Yeah. But it 'ad two collars!'

13 The Criminal Justice Act of 1967 replaced preventive detention with the 'extended sentence'. Corrective training disappeared altogether.

14 In 1954 of a total of 31,274 prisoners received into custody on conviction only 262 men and eight women were under sentence of preventive detention; the figures for corrective training were 502 and 22 respectively (*Report of the Commissioners of Prisons for the Year 1955*, London HMSO, 1956, Cmnd 10).

15 The question of judicial corporal punishment had been explored by the Cadogan Committee in 1938 which had found the evidence of reconvictions to cast grave doubts on its efficacy as a deterrent. The courts had been making progressively less use of it since 1930.

16 *Report* (London, HMSO, 1956, Cmnd 10), appendix 5, table D.

17 Some were run by police officers, others by prison officers in their spare time.

18 The last executions to take place were those of Peter Allen and Gwyn Evans hanged at Liverpool and Manchester on 13 August 1964. See Elwyn Jones, *The Last Two to Hang* (London, Macmillan, 1966).

19 The case of Edith Thompson, hanged with her lover, Arthur Bywaters, was especially tragic. The fancifully hyperbolic language of her love letters, in which she sought to be free of her less than admirable husband, were the source of her eventual destruction. She had to be carried, screaming hysterically, to her execution on 9 January 1923. Her last hours were shared by Margery Fry who had obtained permission to visit her in the death cell. It is a measure of the tragedy that Margery Fry could remember the details for more than 30 years and in a broadcast in 1957 (when she was 81) reflected upon 'feeling her way' towards this 'flimsy personality' ('The Last Things', BBC Home Service, 12 May 1957).

20 James Christoph, *Capital Punishment and British Politics* (London, Allen and Unwin, 1962).
21 Herbert Morrison was himself the son of a London policeman. He eventually came round to the abolitionist cause, as did Chuter Ede.
22 With the exception of the debates, on the Homicide Bill of 1956–7, the issue of the death penalty has always been the subject of a free vote.
23 155 HL Debs, cols 485–92, 28 April 1948.
24 458 HC Debs, col. 565, 18 November 1948.
25 Gowers, a distinguished retired civil servant and the author of *Plain Words* and *The ABC of Plain Words*, subsequently became an abolitionist. See Ernest Gowers, *A Life for a Life* (London, Chatto and Windus, 1956). Graham Harrison was a career civil servant seconded from the Home Office whose outstanding grasp of the issues undoubtedly contributed to the stature of the report which in both language and scholarship is easily the equal of any of the great Victorian 'blue books'.
26 *Report* (London, HMSO 1953, Cmnd 8932).
27 The majority of prison medical officers at this time, including those who prepared reports on prisoners liable to execution, had no qualifications in psychological medicine. The Criminal Justice Act 1948 had regularized the position regarding mental reports, permitting them to be made by a 'medical practitioner qualified or *experienced in* the treatment of mental disorders' (author's italics). Simply having dealt with mentally disordered prisoners in the course of their sentences became regarded as sufficient 'experience'.
28 Throughout the period from 1948 to final abolition there was an undertone of great hostility in the abolitionist camp towards those who had been in office in 1948 and were held to have let a golden opportunity slip by as well as towards judges of the calibre of Goddard.
29 In private conversation with myself and Louis Blom-Cooper, QC subsequent to the passing of the 1957 Act.
30 *Report*, p. 278.
31 Chapter 4, notes 19–20.
32 One body, which had been there since 1943, was found in the back garden. Mrs Christie was under the floorboards and the assorted remains of four prostitutes were stacked in a cupboard under the stairs. There have been several books on the case, the best of which remains Ludovic Kennedy, *Ten Rillington Place* (London, 1961).

33 *Inquiry into the Case of R. v. Evans and the Case of R. v. Christie* (London, HMSO, 1953, Cmnd 8896).
34 The Case of Timothy John Evans. Report of an Inquiry by the Hon. Mr Justice Brabin. Cmnd 3101. October 1966.
35 536 HC Debs, col. 2090, 19 February 1955.
36 The proposal owed much to a publication of Conservative lawyers that had appeared a week or so before. The Inns of Court Conservative and Unionist Society, *Some Suggestions for the Reform of the Law relating to Murder in England* (London, 1956).
37 S.2(1) of the Act states: 'Where a person kills or is a party to the killing of another, he shall not be convicted of murder if he was suffering from such abnormality of mind (whether arising from a condition of arrested or retarded development of mind or any inherent causes or induced by disease or injury) as substantially impaired his mental responsibility for his acts and omissions in doing or being a party to the killing.'

S.2(2) laid the burden of proof of diminished responsibility on the defence and S.2(3) provided for a verdict of manslaughter should the defence succeed.
38 S.3. Within three years of the execution of Ruth Ellis, Ernest Fantle, who had shot his wife's lover after verbal provocation, was convicted of manslaughter and sentenced by Mr Justice Salmon to three years imprisonment under this section. It seems inconceivable that a jury would not have found for provocation in Ruth Ellis's case, though the sentence would have depended greatly on the personality of the trial judge. See Terence Morris and Louis Blom-Cooper, *A Calendar of Murder* (London, Michael Joseph, 1964).
39 S.4 of the Act.
40 Even these have not ceased in cases involving murder; the guilt of the six convicted of the Birmingham pub bombings in 1974, whose plea for a retrial was dismissed by the House of Lords in April 1988, is in considerable doubt, not least with respect to the forensic evidence. In January 1989, the Home Secretary, Douglas Hurd, referred the cases of those convicted of the Guildford and Woolwich pub bombings to the Court of Appeal following representations by the Archbishop of Canterbury, Dr Runcie, the Archbishop of Westminster, Cardinal Hume, two former Home Secretaries, Roy Jenkins and Merlyn Rees, and two former Lords of Appeal, Scarman and Devlin.

7 The Growth of Crime, 1960–1988

That crime should have increased during the war did not come as a particular surprise to those who were closest to the problem. The resources of the police were stretched and it was assumed that wartime conditions would have presented not only more practical opportunities for crime but would, in some degree, have eroded the values and standards of behaviour that had guaranteed a degree of honesty and respect for the persons and property of others. A problem for the social analyst of crime in Britain since the war is to determine a proper base year for comparison. It was natural that the year 1938 was taken in the immediate post-war period as the bench-mark of comparison but, with distance from that year, the comparisons become progressively less useful.

The wartime increase, as shown in chapter 3, had been substantial, of the order of 70 per cent for indictable offences known to the police. But, in real terms, this was only an increase from about 280,000 to just under 480,000 offences; contemporary observers were concerned initially with the magnitude of the increase and then tended to perceive the size of the crime problem as if it too, in absolute terms, was enormous. By present-day standards, it was nothing of the sort; in 1985, for example, no fewer than 3.4 million offences were recorded. It was because crime readily featured as a newspaper staple that references were made to a 'crime wave' when the matter was debated in Parliament, or when judges pronounced on what they perceived to be an astonishing increase in the incidence of a particular type of offence. The streets of British cities in 1945 were almost certainly safer places than they had been in 1845 and were scarcely more dangerous than in 1935.

From table 7.1 it can be seen that in each of the years 1945, 1950, 1955 and 1960 the total number of offences was still less than 750,000 and that the quinquennial percentage variation was actually a minus value between 1945 and 1955. These five-year periods mask the fact that in 1951, the peak year for crime in the post-war period, the number of recorded offences rose to 524,000; thereafter, the numbers fell back until 1955 when they again began to rise. The gross increases were quite small and it was not until 1960 that crime began to move upwards above the three-quarter million mark. Crime reached the million mark in 1964 and the two million mark in 1975, passing three million in 1982. The year 1960 is a key year: by showing an increase of approximately 70 per cent on the preceding five years – similar to the wartime increase between 1938 and 1945 – it demonstrates that it was the late 1950s that saw the true beginnings of the modern crime problem.

Leaving aside for the moment the question of whether the statistics represent the true total of all offences, an increase can come about in one of three ways: (a) a given population is responsible for more offences; (b) an increased population is committing offences at the same rate; (c) an increased population is committing offences at an increased rate. What we can examine is increases in population size and make estimates of a rate of crime per million of population. These data are given in table 7.1, and again it is in the second half of the 1950s that the crime *rate* as distinct from the crude total of offences begins to ascend with serious implications, the quinquennial variation being of the order of 65 per cent.

The inter-war period was, *par excellence*, a period of declining rates of population growth. A substantial number of young men of marriageable age had been killed in the First World War, leaving a larger than normal number of unmarried women in the population, while the effects of the economic depression of the period 1929–34 included a further fall in the number of births. It was a period of the 'one child' or 'no child' family with the result that the number of children and young persons in the population, who constitute the most crime-prone age group, was comparatively low. With the onset of war, the birth

Table 7.1 Indictable offences known to the police, 1945–85

Year	Total offences	Variation over preceding 5 years (%)	Rate per million of population [a]	Variation over preceding 5 years (%)
1945	478,394	+56.8[b]	12,705.3	+30.7[c]
1950	461,435	−3.6	12,097.2	−4.8
1955	438,085	−5.1	11,234.7	−4.8
1960	743,713	+69.8	18,474.1	+64.4
1965	1,133,882	+52.5	28,258.7	+53.0
1970[d]	1,555,995	+37.2	38,030.9	+34.6
1975	2,105,031	+35.3	50,350.1	+32.4
1980	2,520,600	+19.7	58,811.9	+16.8
1985	3,426,400	+35.9	78,204.7	+33.0

[a] Based on a population over the age of criminal responsibility: up to 31 January 1964 eight years, thereafter ten years. Data are calculated on populations appropriately adjusted.
[b] Percentage increase on a 1940 figure of 305,114.
[c] Percentage increase on an annual average rate per million 1940–4 of 9,721.8.
[d] This includes a very large percentage increase for 1969 over 1968, partly due to changes in the law of theft (Theft Act 1968). This was a rise of 15.5 per cent, over twice the rise in the preceding year and more than three times the increase in the following year. If the figures are adjusted to make the 1968 data comparable with the following year, the percentage increase would have been 6.3 per cent. See *Criminal Statistics England and Wales 1970* (London HMSO, 1971, Cmnd 4708), p. xxv.
[e] The data for 1980 are not comparable with preceding years because of changes made by the new counting rules introduced at the beginning of 1980 to improve the consistency of the police of the recording of multiple, continuous and repeated offences.
Source: Criminal Statistics England and Wales, 1950–85 (London, HMSO)

rate began to increase, reaching a 'bulge' in the immediate post-war period 1945–7 when returning servicemen were reunited with their wives and fiancées.

It was Leslie Wilkins, probably the Home Office's most talented statistician of the post-war years, who first explored the phenomenon of the increased criminality of young people.[1] Between 1938 and 1944 the proportion of offenders in the 8–17 age group had increased by about 70 per cent in the case of boys and about 120 per cent in that of girls.[2] Wilkins explored the possibility that a generation of children growing up in wartime had a greater tendency to commit offences, and his data suggested that those cohorts who passed through their fifth year during the war were the most crime-prone 'delinquent generation'. Thus, in 1955, the oldest of this delinquent generation would have been 15 and the youngest 10, and by 1960, 20 and 15 respectively. If Wilkins's theory is considered demonstrated by the increases in the rates per million of population then the effect of the war had been to reduce in some way the effectiveness of social controls over these youngsters.

At this point it is worth considering some of the sociological aspects of the question. The war was a period of maximum disruption in family life; fathers were away in the forces, mothers employed for long hours on war work, and children often left to their own devices and not infrequently indulged by their mothers and grandparents by way of compensation. Large numbers of children were evacuated from their own homes altogether. Certainly, there is some reason to believe that childhood in wartime provided a greater experience if not of freedom then at least of autonomy. These facts were deeply impressed upon those who were most concerned with problems of juvenile delinquency. D. H. Stott, in a study of 102 delinquent boys in an approved school, estimated that no fewer than 19 of them had backgrounds in which the war had played the critical part in the origins of their law-breaking.[3] Among juvenile court magistrates there was a firmly held belief that since so many children in court appeared to come from broken homes domestic disharmony and marriage breakdown must be a cause of delinquency. There was no way of knowing, of course, whether delinquents were a minority in the total population of children from broken or unhappy homes. It was also widely believed that the cinema, to which many children habitually resorted on a Saturday morning for special children's shows, was a potential stimulant of delinquency, as might be 'horror comics' and television.[4]

The difficulty with the 'delinquent generation' argument was that as time passed cohorts of children who were born after the war began to exhibit involvement in crime at an even greater rate. By 1970, the number of crimes per million population was more than twice the 1960 figure. Different arguments then began to be advanced. It had been long held that poverty, in its extremes, was almost certainly a cause of crime and in the mid-nineteenth century this certainly had plausibility as an explanation of the behaviour of those members of a dispossessed underclass for whom the only others options were the workhouse or starvation. Even during the 1930s 'genuine need' had been recognized as a cause of subsistence crime. But, as the standard of living in Britain rose during the second half of the 1950s, so the spectre of poverty largely disappeared into the mists of history and the recollections of those who had suffered in the depression years of the 1930s. It was a paradox that, as the combination of increased national prosperity and the enveloping security of a welfare state seemed to push poverty and deprivation into an increasingly remote past, crime, and especially the crime of the young, seemed inexorably to increase.

The years immediately after the war had been years of austerity with a shortage of consumer goods, in part the result of an emphasis on the export 'drive' that sought to restore national finances which had been severely eroded by the expenses of war – especially the balance of payments. The end of the war had, however, brought some relief in as far as clothing was concerned. Fashions responded; the 'new look' in women's dress took hemlines lower than they had been since 1918 and men's trousers sported turn-ups of up to 22 in. (61 cm) in circumference. By the mid-1950s austerity had given way to prosperity, no small part of which was related to full employment which, with an increasing gross national product, ensured the poorest sections of the population a power to consume that they had hitherto only enjoyed during the wartime years of 1914–18 and 1939–45, was now part of a peacetime reality. Above all, young people had more money in their pockets than ever before and the explosion of a youth culture in the mid-1950s was symbolized in the emergence of a new form of popular music.[5] When, in 1955, the film *Rock around the Clock* was shown in British cinemas the youthful audiences took to the aisles and began to dance the new steps that were known as 'jive'.[6] In some cinemas seats were torn up in the excitement.

The press publicity given to such events confirmed certain stereotypes about young people, associating their leisure activities with delinquency and antisocial behaviour generally. As young people had more money to spend, so the expanding market in consumer goods increasingly targeted them.[7] Gramophone records, record players and clothes were goods that had a specific appeal to the young in that they were the essential equipment of this new and increasingly classless culture. By the 1960s youth culture was having an effect upon large areas of social life; 'groups' spawned almost weekly, radio and television carried programmes indicating the 'top of the pops' and a second stage of a sartorial revolution took place. Overseas visitors spoke of 'Swinging London' and the financial success of the Liverpudlian Beatles was accompanied by the award of the MBE.

Among the older generation, especially those given to assuming the role of moral entrepreneurs, the new youth culture found little favour.[8] Its hedonistic qualities were excoriated and depicted as being at the roots of delinquency. The middle-aged and middle class felt that the source of the trouble was that young people had 'too much money in their pockets'.

The impact of the new youth culture had its effect upon the character of a good deal of criminological research. Where previously studies of intelligence and individual pathology had been pre-eminent, attention now turned to the social context of crime and delinquency.[9] The idea that poverty could be a cause of crime has at least some plausibility, but the notion that an excess of money can be is less easy to appreciate. The 'anti-hedonists' took the view that indulgence in consumer goods produced a sapping of moral fibre. Objections were made to the growing fashion among young males of wearing their hair long. Conscription, which had come to an end by the early 1960s, was seen in retrospect as an institution that had given young men a sense of 'discipline' and 'purpose'. There were frequent calls for the return of conscription throughout the 1960s to deal with delinquency.[10] In approved schools and Detention Centres the staff often went to some trouble to ensure that the inmates had military length 'short back and sides' and that boots replaced fancy Italian footwear. (This is ironic in the light of future fashions among delinquents which were to include semi-shaven heads, heavy boots and jackets and trousers modelled on army combat gear.)

Much of what was taken as indicative of delinquency in this youth culture was relatively harmless in its social consequences and distinctly lucrative for the fashion and recorded music industries. But because many delinquents subscribed to its concerns the error most frequently made was to equate the contemporary youth culture with the culture of delinquency.

In spite of the widespread affluence that characterized British society in the late 1950s and for most of the 1960s, it was not always as totally enveloping as it appeared. Downes, in his study of Stepney, found that many of the traditional cultural features of life in a long-deprived dockland area, such as petty theft, were persistent; he also found that the youths he studied were often aimless and bored, living essentially for the moment and scarcely ever planning for their futures.[11] Since work opportunities were in abundance, they often failed to take it seriously. What Downes's study indicated, along with others at the time, was that the educational system was in no way meeting the needs of young people in a changing world. If anything, the Secondary Modern Schools, to which those who had failed the 'eleven plus' selection were consigned, reinforced a sense of unequal social opportunity at the very time when at the other end of the scale higher education was in the process of expanding. The Secondary Moderns were publicly identified with failure but were divisive not simply on this account, but because they provided no new opportunities or challenges to the children despatched to them. The enthusiasm for comprehensive schools was born of a desire that was both egalitarian and functional, for in the 'new' society of the 1960s with its emphasis on technology, a sub-literate and sub-numerate labour force, fit only to be the hewers of wood and drawers of water, had no place.[12] It can be argued that there was, in fact, a much more plausible explanation for the increase in crime after 1955 – related to the concept of 'crime as opportunity'.[13]

Crime in the emergent consumer society

From table 7.2 it can be seen that crimes against property, which had actually fallen in the decade 1945–55, began

Table 7.2 Selected indictable offences known to the police, 1945–85

Year	Violence against the person	Variation over preceding 5 years (%)	Offences against property [a]	Variation over preceding 5 years (%)	Sexual offences	Variation over preceding 5 years (%)
1945	4,743	+95.7[b]	454,830	+55.8[c]	8,546	+84.7[d]
1950	6,249	+31.8	427,061	−6.1	13,185	+54.3
1955	7,884	+26.2	399,924	−6.4	17,078	+29.5
1960	15,759	+99.9	688,381	+72.1	19,937	+16.7
1965	25,549	+62.1	1,064,602	+54.7	20,155	+1.1
1970	41,088	+60.8	1,464,976	+37.6	24,163	+19.9
1975	71,002	+72.8	1,923,907	+31.3	23,731	−1.8
1980[e]	97,246	+37.0	2,206,368	+14.7	21,107	−11.1
1985	121,700	+25.1	2,917,700	+32.2	21,500	+1.9

[a] From 1945 to 1948 offences against property included larceny, breaking and entering, receiving, frauds and false pretences. After the Theft Act 1968, the category was expanded to include burglary, robbery, theft, handling stolen goods, fraud and forgery.
[b] Percentage increase on 1940 figure of 2,424.
[c] Percentage increase on 1940 figure of 292,008.
[d] Percentage increase on 1940 figure of 4,626.
[e] Data for 1980 are not comparable with preceding years because of changes made by the new counting rules introduced at the beginning of 1980 to improve the consistency of the police of the recording of multiple, continuous and repeated offences.
Source: Criminal Statistics England and Wales, 1950–85 (London, HMSO)

substantially to increase after that date, the steepest rise of 72 per cent occurring in the quinquennium 1955–60. This was, of course, the period in which the emphasis in the post-war economy shifted from domestic austerity and concentration on the export market to the development of the home market as part of the total phenomenon of economic growth. The most striking change, in the sense of its high visibility, was the availability of motor vehicles. In 1955 many of the vehicles and especially private cars on the road had been built in the 1930s; new cars were notoriously hard to come by since most were destined for export. But by this time the motor industry had begun to redesign most of its models and offer them in increasing numbers on the home market which was becoming more buoyant as more people had the wherewithal to buy a car. As the ownership of cars and motorcycles rapidly expanded, greatly in excess of the available off-street garaging space, so more attractive targets for theft came into view. By the mid-1960s thefts of and from motor vehicles as well as the offence of 'take and drive'[14] greatly increased. By the 1960s ordinary people simply owned more property than they had ever done before.[15] The transistor had made wireless sets highly portable, the new long-playing gramophone record used with the new transistorized record players were equally portable and, after the Coronation of 1953 (a key stimulus for sales), the falling relative price of television sets and the expansion of television rental companies meant that what had previously been something available only to the fairly well off was now, like the refrigerator and the washing machine, becoming a normal item of household equipment. The increase in the volume of such property, much of it small in relation to its value, has to be seen against the increase in property crime. For in an important sense, property crime is a form of redistribution of goods. The thief steals an item and takes it to a 'fence' or professional receiver who will buy it from him at a substantial discount. He in turn will sell it on, making a small profit, but at a price which is substantially below the legitimate market price.[16] Some thieves will sell directly to others, usually in pubs, but there is a steady flow of merchandise through professional fences which reaches down to the entrepreneurs on the market stalls who offer goods of what appear to be high quality at relatively low prices.[17]

Innovations in the pattern of merchandising in the late 1950s produced changes in the opportunities for crime. Previously, the basic layout of almost all shops had consisted of a substantial counter, behind which a large number of shop assistants were ranged, to divide the shopper from the goods which were piled on shelves against the wall. The changes followed developments in the United States where shops were being transformed into 'supermarkets'. The aim of the supermarket was twofold: to reduce labour costs by introducing a system of 'self-service' by the customer from island counters and shelves to which there was unrestricted access, and to increase the volume of sales by allowing the customer to handle the goods, often being stimulated by 'impulse' purchases of goods displayed in a place visible to the queue at the check-out counter. A few shops, notably Woolworths and Marks and Spencer had always displayed their goods on counters *between* the customer and the shop assistant, but the explosion of supermarkets in the grocery trade suddenly increased the vulnerability of goods in shops.

By the 1960s thefts from shops had become an established feature of retailing, although not a great deal was known about the shoplifters themselves.[18] Some, it was assumed, were professionals and others juveniles. But one group that attracted some attention were the offenders who clearly had the means to pay for the goods and seemed to be in some personal crisis.[19] Both police officers and magistrates frequently criticized the open counter system as putting temptation in the way of offenders, especially children, and there is little doubt but that the arrangement provides a ready opportunity for theft.[20] Shops, on the other hand, despite the employment of private detectives, have recognized that the advantages of the supermarket are greater than the disadvantages of theft and the costs of private policing.[21]

A second method of marketing derived from the United States was the self-service petrol filling station. The pressures here seem to have been exclusively the need to reduce labour costs as the retail price of road fuel offered smaller and smaller profit margins. Self-service petrol stations have had their problems of crime, the earliest being the phenomenon of the 'drive out' in which the car driver, having filled his tank, then makes off at high speed leaving the cashier impotent in the pay-booth.

In recent years it has become necessary to provide the cashiers with a form of defensible space to protect them against attack and robbery, especially late at night.[22]

Crimes of disorder

More perplexing has been the growth of violent crime. Again, it was the quinquennium 1955–60 that saw the greatest proportional increase (of 100 per cent), but between 1960 and 1965 violence continued to increase. It has to be considered in relation to other forms of crime and, contrary to popular belief, the chances of becoming a victim of violence are neither as great nor as widespread as is generally supposed. What is also true is that while such offences continue to increase, the rate of increase appears to be falling. *The British Crime Survey* indicated that both victims and offenders in personal violence tend to be young lower-class males who spend a substantial part of their leisure time drinking in public houses.[23] The association of violent behaviour with alcohol and alcohol abuse has been long known to criminologists, and it plays a not insignificant part in criminal homicide and the physical abuse of women and children. There is also some reason to think that it can be associated with other offences of petty theft and vandalism.

When interpreting the statistics, it has to be borne in mind that they reflect attitudes to law enforcement as much as the incidence of the offences themselves. The growth of television journalism, and with it a greater public awareness of social issues, has undoubtedly increased public consciousness of violent behaviour, especially in a group setting. Violence at football matches is by no means a novel phenomenon and was known at grounds like Millwall in the 1920s; trouble there did not, however, disturb the national newspaper headlines and scarcely reached the *Kentish Mercury* unless a court case ensued. At Easter 1964 groups of youngsters caused trouble in the Essex resort of Clacton on Sea; the weather was cold and rainy and it would seem that boredom set in early. The conflict focused on hostility between groups of 'Mods' riding motor scooters and 'Rockers' on large conventional motorcycles. The arcane distinctions between Mod and Rocker culture were exemplified in their dress. Since little else happened in Britain that wet Bank Holiday Monday, the trouble at Clacton became a front-page story.

In *Folk Devils and Moral Panics*, Stanley Cohen describes how, when young people went to other seaside resorts at Whitsun, they sought out a role to play which the press had readily provided for them, while the police and, in particular, the lay magistracy, were already prepared for what was styled the 'invasion of the beaches'.[24] When there was trouble, police intervention was swift and magisterial justice severe. Some magistrates, like the Chairman of the Margate bench, a Dr Simpson, went to great lengths to castigate defendants for their behaviour, often in language which was beyond their comprehension, referring to them as 'petty sawdust Caesars'. But the problem with the 'moral panic' (as Cohen terms it) which had been created was that it had a quality of self-perpetuation. Seaside disturbances became the order of the day at Bank Holidays around the country for the next two years.

The emergence of racial conflicts

Violent crime also took other and more sinister forms. By the mid-1950s immigration from the British West Indies in response to a demand for labour resulted in the settlement of numbers of people of Afro-Caribbean descent in London and a number of other centres. In London the original concentration of this settlement was in the Notting Hill district of North Kensington, a run down area that had been the setting for Christie's multiple murders. In August 1958 a number of white youths mounted an attack on a group of West Indians; the fracas became a running battle through the streets and a number of serious injuries were sustained as the result of the use of various offensive weapons. There had been earlier disturbances that month in Nottingham where white youths had attacked blacks and again on the same night as the trouble in Notting Hill. Both the Metropolitan Police Commissioner and the Home Secretary took a serious view of these events, and in the case of those at Notting Hill the matter went to be tried at the Old Bailey before Mr Justice Salmon who handed down what were, for 1958, very severe sentences of up to six years' imprisonment. As such, these events were seen as a reminder of the troubles that had afflicted Glasgow and Liverpool in the 1930s when gangs of youths, some calling themselves Protestant, others Catholic, sought each other out in the context of communal strife. Although serious racial disturbances ceased after the Notting Hill sentences – it was widely believed on account of the nature of the sentences handed down – racial incidents did not altogether disappear and by the late 1970s were becoming frequent, often associated with the activities of 'skinheads', the youths who had taken over in part the mantle of the 'Rockers' in their aggressive appearance and militaristic dress but with an altogether uglier and more sinister political philosophy.

The growth of drug abuse

Moral panics associated with violence did not disappear. Towards the end of the 1960s less attention was being paid to the subject of violence and more concern was being shown about the growing phenomenon of drug abuse. It had arisen from the growth of cannabis use which had become popular among young people, mainly of middle-class origin. Smoking 'pot' became part of a hedonistic culture that flourished as part of the predominant youth culture. It owed much to the 'Flower Power' movement on the West Coast of the USA which combined a stated desire for pacific behaviour ('peace and love') with the pursuit of bodily pleasure. Where the students at the University of California, Berkeley, had invented the 'sit-in' as a form of social protest, the Flower People practised 'love-ins'. Cannabis was the staple drug, but it was soon joined by LSD, an infinitely more dangerous substance.

In dealing with the drug phenomenon, the Wilson government had to allay public anxiety but was unwilling to take the kinds of restrictive steps that were being used in the United States. It legislated in 1967 but as the same time encouraged the Advisory Council on the Penal System to examine the problem. Certainly, the demand for cannabis, and later for heroin, had its effects upon crime, not, as in the United States, by driving large numbers of drug-dependent individuals to commit violent crime on the street to get the cash with which to finance their habit, but, rather, in the form of providing a profitable area of activity for professional and organized criminals.

The drug problem has changed its social profile since the 1960s. Whereas middle-class students used cannabis, working-class youngsters employed manufactured drugs that the pharmaceutical industry had created to deal with medical conditions, involving the abuse of amphetamines and barbiturates. Supplies of these drugs were often obtained by the burglary of retail pharmacies; blank pads of prescription forms were sometimes stolen from doctors' surgeries and used with success in obtaining drugs on the basis of fraudulent and forged prescriptions.[25]

Racial harassment, vandalism and declining civilities

Other changes in the nature of crime since 1945 have reflected a diminution in the civilities of life in public places. For, although the ordinary citizen's chances of being violently assaulted and robbed in a public place are on average extremely slim, the average does not necessarily reflect the picture in particular areas. Thus a young Bangladeshi in the Spitalfields district of East London is wise to take care of himself if he goes about alone at certain times since there is always the possibility that local 'skinheads' may decide that the time is ripe to give their racial sentiments another practical expression. Women in the run-down areas of inner cities may eschew going out at night since they fear assault on the unlit landings and walkways of public housing estates. Lonely tunnels and platforms on the underground railway may also be areas of high vulnerability.

Even without the threat of physical attack, the effects of vandalism are everywhere to be seen and not only in urban areas. The commonest target of vandalism has been the telephone kiosk, the 1930s design being wholly vulnerable to having its coinbox opened, its equipment smashed and its windows broken; no other item of street furniture has suffered with such social consequences. But other vulnerable targets such as bus shelters have also suffered, including those in rural areas which suggests that the theory that vandalism is a response to the deprivations of the urban environment is not entirely plausible.

The term 'vandalism', like 'mugging', has no meaning in criminal law, the concept being that of criminal damage. Before the Criminal Damage Act of 1971 the data are hard to classify since prosecutions could be brought under two distinct acts, one of 1861 and one of 1914, depending upon the kind of property involved and the nature of the penalty, the prosecutor thought appropriate.[26] Since 1971 the situation has been codified, but the figures before 1977 exclude damage to property under £20 in value (see table 7.3). *The British Crime Survey* estimated that less than 10 per cent of cases are reported to the police, and various local surveys suggest that a great deal of minor vandalism is the work of children some of whom may be below the age of criminal responsibility. The same is also true of the placing of heavy objects on railway tracks and the throwing of missiles at trains.

Explanations of crime: poverty and unemployment

If poverty was considered a cause of crime in the pre-war period and affluence at the root of it in the boom times of the 1960s, the theory that has emerged in the 1980s is that of unemployment. The situation is complicated by a number of factors relating to the duration of unemployment in individual cases, the age groups involved and the circumstances in which unemployment arises. Thus, for example, a recent study of the effects of the closing of the steel works in Corby, when a significant proportion of the whole town's workforce found itself redundant, found that those offenders detected in crime were people who had often been in trouble before and only a minority among them were ex-steel workers.[27] The latter, however, became increasingly vulnerable as *victims* when they began to spend their redundancy money on items that were the targets of household burglary.

Given that the young are more prone to crime than the middle-aged, any increase in youth unemployment is likely to have a greater effect than in the case of older workers. At the

Table 7.3 Offences of Criminal Damage 1975–85

Year	*Arson*	*Criminal damage endangering life*	*Other criminal damage*	*Threat to commit criminal damage*	*Total*
1975[a]	7,468	85	70,473[d]	520	78,546[b]
1976[a]	7,713	140	84,764[d]	425	93,042[b]
1977[a]	9,415	92	287,391[b]	475	297,373[b]
			113,899[c]		123,881[c]
1978[a]	10,702	112	295,054[b]	404	306,272[b]
			129,312[c]		140,530[c]
1979[a]	11,640	98	308,199[b]	532	320,469[b]
			148,128[c]		160,398[c]
1980	13,585	92	345,268[b]	505	359,450[b]
			177,661[c]		191,843[c]
1981	15,116	68	370,917[b]	626	386,727[b]
			201,377[c]		217,187[c]
1982	16,134	84	400,966[b]	630	417,814[b]
			226,880[c]		243,728[c]
1983	17,121	82	425,553[b]	560	443,316[b]
			249,496[c]		267,259[c]
1984	18,889	112	478,152[b]	687	497,840[b]
			292,852[c]		312,540[c]
1985	19,003	97	519,050[b]	814	538,964[b]
			333,600[c]		353,514[c]

[a] Figures for 1980 onwards not comparable with those for previous years due to changes in recording multiple, continous and repeated offences.
[b] Including damage to property valued at £20 or less.
[c] Excluding damage to property valued at £20 or less.
[d] Excluding damage to property valued at £20 or less.
Source: Criminal Statistics England and Wales, 1975–85 (London, HMSO)

Scarman Inquiry into the Brixton disorders in 1981 it was accepted that the rate of unemployment for black people in the area was around 25 per cent compared with an estimate of 13 per cent for whites, while for young black males under 19 years the estimate was 55 per cent.[28] Unfortunately, because unemployment has become such a politically charged theme, the distinction between the idea of unemployment being a *cause* of crime as distinct from some excuse or justification for it has not always clearly emerged in the public debate. By no means all unemployed black youths in Brixton in 1981 were committing crime any more than all of them were rioting in the streets: in that sense unemployment is not 'causative' in any inexorable sense of the term. What it may do, however, is to act in conjunction with other aspects of social and economic deprivation both to lessen any commitment to the conventional social order and to make any opportunity to commit crime seem more attractive. Long days of idleness are scarcely conducive to a sense of constructive fulfilment and, as we know from studies such as Downes's, boredom is often a factor in petty crime. What may be more important is that unemployment is relevant as a dimension of deprivation as a whole. By and large, the unemployed, especially the young, are very poor and, like others among the very poor, may be tempted to commit offences that are relevant to their poverty.[29]

The correlation between unemployment and crime is complex and uncertain, though it clearly exists. The correlation between unemployment and increased imprisonment, by contrast, is quite clear. Not only are unemployed offenders individually more likely to receive custodial sentences than those in work, but analyses of the population of institutions indicates that unemployment cannot be discounted as a factor in determining admission rates.[30] The best discussion of the problem of crime and unemployment is contained in a recent (and sadly posthumous) publication of Steven Box.[31] To understand the precise nature of the relationship will require more research into wider areas of social change in British society, including the possibility that the new 'post-industrial' society will both contain and need to accommodate an equivalent of the Victorian 'underclass'. That group will consist of individuals who, unable to compete effectively for jobs, and thereby for housing and other essential commodities, will become increasingly dependent upon public welfare; but if, as seems likely, the scope and magnitude of public welfare progressively diminishes, then it will need to resort either to crime or to street trade (or a combination of the two).

Responses to crime

Public and government responses to the growth of crime over the past 40 years have been characterized by a perceptible shift in the methods thought to be most fruitful in containing and reducing crime. The mood of both government and public in the late 1940s was characterized by the view that certainty of detection was the best deterrent and that once detected various penal methods would bring about a change of heart in the offender, whether by punishment or rehabilitation. The period of optimism about the control of crime probably reached its height in the mid-1960s. By the 1970s, a mood of pessimism had set in, stimulated by the recognition that even if rehabilitation 'worked' it would be working on so few – by reason of the small proportion of offenders who were apprehended – that it would make hardly a dent in the problem. The enthusiasm then shifted to the idea of physical methods of crime prevention that targeted *all* potential offenders. For this reason the future social historians may make mention of the last decades of the twentieth century as the time when the modern locksmith, aided by all the advantages of microchip electronics, came into his own.

Notes

1 Leslie T. Wilkins, *Delinquent Generations. Studies in the Causes of Delinquency and the Treatment of Offenders*, no. 3 (Home Office, HMSO, 1960). The Criminal Justice Act 1948 had made public financial provision for criminological research for the first time.

2 Hermann Mannheim, *Comparative Criminology*, vol. 2 (London, Routledge and Kegan Paul, 1965), p. 598.

3 D. H. Stott. *Delinquency and Human Nature*. Dunfermline. Carnegie United Kingdom Trust. 1950.

4 A Departmental Committee on Children and the Cinema was set up in 1946. Mannheim cites numerous studies of the effects of the cinema and comic books including the pioneering study by Hilde Himmelweit, A. N. Oppenheim and Pamela Vince, *Television and the Child* (London, Tavistock, 1958). See Mannheim, *Comparative Criminology*, pp. 603–4.

5 Bill Haley and his group 'The Comets' became a transnational phenomenon in 1955.

6 During the war a new dance rhythm known as 'jitterbugging' became popular at the time of the 'big bands' like those of Glenn Miller. Although popular among US servicemen and their British girlfriends, notices prohibiting it appeared in many commercial dance halls whose management insisted on the decorum associated with the *thé dansant* until the early 1950s. The film *Rock around the Clock* appeared in 1955 and Elvis Presley's first successful record *Heartbreak Hotel* was issued in 1956.

7 Mark Abrams, *The Teenage Consumer* (London, London Press Exchange, 1959).

8 See Timothy Raison (ed.), *Youth in New Society* (London, Rupert Hart-Davis, 1966).

9 John Mays was a pioneer in this field with *Growing Up in the City* (Liverpool, Liverpool University Press, 1954), which was followed by *On the Threshold of Delinquency* (Liverpool, Liverpool University Press, 1959) and *Education and the Urban Child* (Liverpool, Liverpool University Press, 1962). *The Young Pretenders* (London, Michael Joseph) appeared in 1965. For a review of the research of this period, see David Downes, *The Delinquent Solution* (London, Routledge and Kegan Paul, 1966).

10 Earlier studies had shown that delinquents, when conscripted, simply became problems for the services. Not infrequently, they were court-martialled, held in military prisons and discharged with ignominy. John C. Spencer, *Crime and the Services* (London, Routledge and Kegan Paul, 1954).

11 David Downes, *The Delinquent Solution*, esp. chapter 7.

12 This is in contrast to earlier periods in which repetitive factory work, physical labouring and domestic service were among the principal features of a labour intensive economy.

13 This notion has been explored by P. Mayhew, R. V. G. Clarke, A. Sturman and J. M. Hough, *Crime as Opportunity* (Home Office Research Study 34, London, HMSO, 1976).

14 Not a theft, since subsequent abandonment of the vehicle meant that there was no intention permanently to deprive the owner of possession – an essential ingredient in the crime of theft.

15 See chapter 8, note 2.

16 See Karl Klockars, *The Professional Fence* (London, Tavistock, 1975).

17 For example, high-quality clothing, which may have been stolen whilst in transit, will reappear without labels or washing instructions and perhaps be described as 'bankrupt stock'.

18 For an excellent account of shop theft and researches into it, see Dermot Walsh, *Shoplifting: Controlling a Major Crime* (London,

MacMillan, 1978).

19 T. C. N. Gibbens and J. Prince, *Shoplifting* (London, Institute for the Study and Treatment of Delinquency, 1962).

20 For example, for young girls to steal make-up and toiletries.

21 'Self-service shops have learnt to adjust to a high level of shoplifting, since it is matched by an even higher sales curve' (Walsh, *Shoplifting*, p. 91).

22 Experiments with machines that would accept paper money were unsuccessful. The advent of the credit card has, however, reduced the amount of vulnerable cash for which lone cashiers may be responsible late at night. Credit card thefts and subsequent frauds have nevertheless emerged as a new crime.

23 M. Hough and P. Mayhew, *The British Crime Survey* (Home Office Research Study 76, London, HMSO, 1983); and Michael Gottfredson, *Victims of Crime: the Dimensions of Risk* (Home Office Research Study 81, London, HMSO, 1984.

24 Stanley Cohen, *Folk Devils and Moral Panics: the Creation of the Mods and Rockers* (London, MacGibbon and Kee, 1972).

25 See Jock Young, *The Drug Takers* (London, MacGibbon and Kee, 1971).

26 Malicious Damage Act 1861 and Criminal Justice Administration Act 1914 S.14(1). There were complex distinctions in the law of property between the two provisions.

27 R. M. Richards, 'An Examination of the Relationship between Crime and Unemployment in Corby'. Unpublished M. Phil. Thesis, University of Nottingham, 1987.

28 Lord Justice Scarman, *The Brixton Disorders* (London, HMSO, 1982, Cmnd 8427).

29 My own experience of two courts in the poorest areas of south London over more than 20 years are that what are technically frauds on the DHSS generally involve very small sums. Similarly, many young women caught shoplifting have been stealing either children's clothes or, at Christmas time, small items to give as presents.

30 F. Gladstone, 'Crime and the crystal ball', *Home Office Research Unit Bulletin*, no. 7, 1979

31 Steven Box, *Recession, Crime and Punishment* (London, Macmillan, 1987).

8 The Reforms of the 1960s

The rejection of Conservatism

The general election of October 1964 brought to an end 13 continuous years of Conservative government, but the Labour administration that took office under Harold Wilson that month was drawn from a party very different from that which had come to power in 1945. Not only had most of the senior ministers of that government long since departed from politics but Aneurin Bevan and Hugh Gaitskell, both potential prime ministers, were dead.[1] The mood of the party was also very different. In 1945 the emphasis had been on social reconstruction and the foundation of what was to become popularly known as the 'welfare state'. In the intervening years much had happened, both inside the Labour party and in British society as a whole.

Within the party, during the opposition years, there had developed a struggle for its 'soul', centring around thc famous Clause Four of the constitution which related to the subject of public ownership. Gaitskell had taken the position that a slavish adherence to principles that had been worked out before the First World War would handicap the party in its appeal to voters in what was by now an affluent society. For the years of Conservative government, whatever else might have been said about them, were a period of economic growth in which wealth had been substantially redistributed downwards, not least through the agencies of education and welfare. Harold Macmillan, the Prime Minister from 1957 to 1963, had told the electorate that they had 'never had it so good'.[2] Nevertheless, there was a disenchantment with a party that had been so long in power; a new generation had grown up remembering nothing of the war except as a fleeting memory of early childhood and it tended to think of the revered figures of the political establishment as being as outmoded as their watch-chains and starched collars.[3] The fashionable mode of transport for the young had become the motor scooter, the Lambretta and the Vespa being the counterparts of the new narrowly cut Italian suits and winkle-picker shoes.

A climate for change

The public mood was again one of expectation, not so much for 'reform' in the traditional sense, but of new and exciting innovation. The Robbins Committee on Higher Education, which was to oversee the greatest period of university expansion that the country had ever known, had been appointed early in 1961. In the United States John F. Kennedy had been elected the youngest ever President and was seen as a symbol of hope and progress by young people in the West.[4] His assassination in 1963 was to be the focus of international grief. In various subtle ways the Labour party under Wilson's leadership capitalized on many of these hopes and emotions and presented the possibility of a society in which the quality of life would continue to be enriched for everyone, this time by the conscious exploitation of the new technologies that were emerging in what was to become known as the 'post-industrial society'.[5]

'Permissiveness' or 'freedom'

It is a current political fashion to think of the 1960s as a decade in which social permissiveness was given free rein with the consequence that there is now a powerful vein of indiscipline in British society. Certainly, a number of reforms were enacted that reduced some of the traditional constraints on individual behaviour of which the legalization of homosexual behavior between consenting adult males in private was among the most controversial. But the legalization of homosexuality was not an invention of the legal reformers of the Wilson era but rather the culmination of a process that had begun 12 years previously when, in response to public concern after a major social scandal, the Eden administration had set up a committee to consider the problem – but had seen fit to do nothing about it.[6] A similar situation applied to the reform of the divorce law. Back in 1937, A. P. Herbert's Bill had tried to abolish the concept of the 'matrimonial offence'; the attempt failed and in 1948 Mrs (later Baroness) Irene White, the Member for Flint tried again to bring the divorce laws into line with contemporary standards. The response of the Attlee administration to what seemed as controversial and politically sensitive an issue as capital punishment was, similarly, to set up a Royal Commission.[7]

A greater contrast between two Royal Commissions would be hard to find. The Chairman of the Commission on Marriage and Divorce, Lord Morton of Henryton was a very different person from Sir Ernest Gowers and, although numerous witnesses from the legal profession gave evidence about the way in which the doctrine of the matrimonial offence led to both absurdity and perjury, the Commissioners clearly preferred the views of those witnesses who considered that any increase in the ease with which divorce was granted would undermine both the institution of the family and personal morality. Indeed, at this period 'broken homes' were widely considered to be a primary cause of juvenile delinquency, and Claud Mullins, a distinguished juvenile magistrate in the London courts, had laid not a little of the blame at the door of the Legal Aid and Advice Act 1949 for making it easier for couples to get into the divorce court.[8]

Between 1964 and 1968 divorce petitions had been running at an average of 40,000 a year, but following the Divorce Law Reform Act of 1969 the figure rose to over 120,000.[9] What the Act did was to provide a ground of 'irretrievable breakdown' making it no longer necessary for the petitioner to establish cruelty or adultery on the part of his or her spouse. Until then, couples whose marriages had genuinely broken down were compelled to make allegations of cruelty or infidelity, whether they were true or not.[10] Difficulty in obtaining a divorce did not ensure that couples did not separate, and it can be argued that the 1967 Act, far from further eroding the foundations of family life as some of the witnesses to the Morton Commission might have supposed, merely allowed couples to end their marriages with greater integrity.

The signs of liberalizing reform were already in evidence before the Wilson government took office. In 1961 the Suicide Act made it no longer an offence for a person to take his own life (it had been a felony since the Middle Ages) nor for a person to attempt suicide. Today, the idea of prosecuting a person, generally in deep depression or distress, for attempting suicide may seem as bizarre as putting someone on trial for witchcraft, but in 1952 just over 500 people were so prosecuted. By 1960, the number had fallen to 60; an indication that changes in thinking about mental illness had taken deep root.[11]

Changes had also been taking place in the law relating to obscenity. Originally an offence under ecclesiastical law, the Victorians had enacted their own legislation in the Obscene Publications Act of 1857. In 1954 the highly respected firm of Martin Secker and Warburg had been prosecuted for publishing a novel, *The Philanderer*, which was held to be obscene on account of its explicit sexual passages. The defendants were fortunate in having an enlightened, if sometimes eccentric, judge Mr Justice Stable,[12] who suggested that the arguments about what was obscene needed to be examined carefully.[13]

The Philanderer case was to be the first of several that were to redefine standards of public taste that fell within the ambit of the criminal law. Although a new Obscene Publications Act was passed in 1959 the subject was far from closed for in 1960 Penguin Books decided to print in Britain an unexpurgated edition of D. H. Lawrence's *Lady Chatterley's Lover*. It had originally appeared abroad in 1928 but no British publisher had dared to issue it for fear of prosecution. By the end of the year the pioneers of paperback publishing were in the dock at the Old Bailey. The publishers were defended by Gerald Gardiner, QC, soon to become Lord Chancellor in the Wilson government of 1964. Here the argument raged around who might be 'corrupted',[14] and Gardiner asked who it was that was corrupted: 'It is always someone else; it is never ourselves.'[15]

But the very acquittal of the publishers of *Lady Chatterley's Lover* on this point led to a difficulty in prosecuting the merchants of common pornography. Two years later in the case of *Clayton* v. *Halsey* an experienced police officer testified that he was not susceptible to depravity or corruption and there was no evidence that the material had been published to a third party.[16] To overcome the difficulties of this case the law was amended in 1964 to cover the question of having an obscene article for publication or gain.

In 1968, by means of the Theatres Act, the government went on to deal with another aspect of the control of obscenity. Since the sixteenth century, it had been the responsibility of an official of the Royal Household, the Lord Chamberlain, to license theatres for public performances. Originally this was certainly a form of political control but during the Victorian period it had become a form of moral censorship, concerned with obscenity and blasphemy. The Act abolished the Lord Chamberlain's powers and subjected theatre performances to the same tests as applied to literature under the Obscene Publications Act of 1959.

It can be argued that, far from facilitating a period of licence that has had deleterious effects upon British society ever since, the course of law reform moved towards the protection of the artistic in literature and the performing arts which should have made it easier to deal with the aesthetically fraudulent and frankly pornographic. In legislating, it attempted to move with the times. The Abortion Act of 1967, a private member's Bill for which the government found time, and the reform of the law relating to adult male homosexuality reflected, too, what were now widely accepted standards of tolerance.

The Longford Committee and its influence

Given that the strategic appeal of the Labour party in the run up to the 1964 election was to 'modernize' Britain, both its economy and society, it was consistent for Wilson to seek advice from various experts in advance. In 1963 he invited a number of individuals with experience in the criminal justice field to join a study group under the chairmanship of the Earl of Longford. The group reported the following year, its conclusions becoming available just as Labour was taking up office.[17] The Longford Committee included some distinguished individuals: Gerald Gardiner, by now as eminent at the Bar as Shawcross had been in the days of Attlee and soon to become Lord Chancellor; Elwyn Jones, QC, about to become Attorney General and a later Lord Chancellor; Bea (later Baroness) Serota, who had been Chairman of the London County Council Children's Committee,[18] and Alice Bacon, who was about to become a junior minster in the Home Office. Longford himself, although his ministerial responsibilities had been in the Control Commission in Germany, in aviation, and were soon to be in the Colonial Office, was an immensely powerful figure in the penal reform movement and had been involved in a number of practical ventures including the New Bridge, a private organization for assisting ex-prisoners.

The Longford Committee effectively settled much of the agenda for reform within the criminal justice system during the first Wilson government. It was concerned with three main issues: reform of the prison system and the services ancillary to it, including sentencing practices in the courts; the treatment of juveniles; and the reform of the law of murder. In retrospect, the Longford group can be seen as breaking new ground, not merely in its deliberations but in the fact that for the first time in the history of the penal reform movement, a political leader who was about to assume power had actually invited the reformers in to advise in advance of legislation. The contrast with the Attlee years is acute for then, if the reformers had any access to the corridors of power, it was almost certainly through their private relationships with senior civil servants. The Howard League had had to organize a Parliamentary Penal Reform Group and present memorials to the Home Secretary; in 1963–4 in a committee room of the House of Lords and at the St Ermine's Hotel in Victoria, future ministers and reformers sat down together. Gardiner had been a key figure in the National Campaign for the Abolition of the Death Penalty and it was not surprising that a Bill to abolish capital punishment was published within the year. Before it became law in November 1965 two amendments were moved.[19] The first by Henry Brooke, a former Home Secretary and now in opposition, required both Houses to declare, by affirmative resolution before 31 July 1970 that the Act be extended, otherwise the law would revert to that contained in the Homicide Act 1957. The second, moved in the Lords by the Lord Chief Justice, Lord Parker, gave judges the power to recommend the minimum period to be served before a person sentenced to life imprisonment for murder could be released.[20] Both Houses affirmatively so resolved in 1969 and there the matter rested until the advent of the Thatcher administration in 1979.

The Criminal Justice Act of 1967

With regard to sentencing and the prison system, the Criminal Justice Act 1967 was to be the source of two major innovations. For years, the criticism had been made that the courts, especially the Magistrates Courts, were too free in sending offenders to prison. The 1967 Act proceeded some way to rectifying this state of affairs by introducing the concept of the suspended sentence. This could be for a maximum of three years and if at any time during that period the offender was again before a court the sentence would automatically take effect unless there were special circumstances.[21] The sentence would be like a sword of Damocles, with only the offender able to cut the silken thread. So far, so good; but by going further and making mandatory the suspension of all sentences of six months or less, the Act effectively removed the power of magistrates to impose any sentence of immediate imprisonment. This provision was highly unpopular and the Magistrates' Association, by now a powerful body, and far removed from the fledgling organization founded by Margery Fry almost half a century before, campaigned ceaselessly until the law was subsequently amended by a subsequent Conservative government.[22] Gardiner, as Lord Chancellor, had done his best to reform the method of appointment to the magistracy, setting up local advisory committees to interview prospective JPs and requiring them to agree to undergo training before taking their seats on the bench. The year 1965 represents an important date in this respect, since when the number of untrained magistrates has fallen almost to zero.[23]

From the criminal statistics for the years 1968–70 it appears that the courts as a whole, and especially the Magistrates Courts, began to pass more prison sentences, albeit suspended, and make proportionately fewer probation orders. This was to have the effect of increasing the prison population, since some offenders would, by further offences, activate their suspended sentences. It was probably a mistake to have made the sentence mandatory for sentences of six months or less, both with regard to the penological consequences and, not least, on account of the ill will it generated among JPs.

The introduction of parole

The second major innovation was the provision of parole for convicted prisoners. Release *on licence* had always existed, but it was at the discretion of the Home Secretary and largely limited to prisoners serving life sentences and juveniles detained at the Sovereign's Pleasure.[24] Under the 1967 Act a prisoner who had served one-third of his sentence or 12 months, whichever was the longer, would be eligible for parole with respect to the unexpired portion of his sentence. Originally it was proposed that recommendations for parole would be made by the prison authorities but considerable pressure was privately exerted on Roy Jenkins, the Home Secretary, to establish an independent review body without which the system had no hope of attaining credibility among prisoners. Surprisingly, the Howard League formed no part of this lobby and appeared content with what was proposed.[25] The aim was to reduce the prison population and at the same time permit the release of those offenders for whom continuing incarceration served no useful purpose, either for them or the community. In its 20 years of existence the system has largely survived its critics, building up an enduring bureaucracy and seldom being embarrassed by serious mistakes. Initially, it was felt that the possibility of parole would encourage the judges in the higher courts to pass longer sentences on the assumption that they would be shortened by parole (which would be by no means certain). A deeper, philosophical criticism, relates to the proposition that executive justice can represent *injustice* if the offender has no way of knowing how to please his captors in order to secure his early release, or if his release is denied on account of factors over which he has no control.[26]

Children in trouble

It was in changing the law dealing with juvenile offenders in the Children and Young Persons Act 1969 that reform was to prove most controversial, raising magisterial hostility to a higher pitch even than the mandatory suspended sentence had done. The Longford Committee had been influenced in its thinking by what was then a current theory in criminology, that of 'labelling'. Impressed by the fact that middle-class children who offended were generally dealt with in informal, non-judicial ways which protected them from the stigma of a juvenile court appearance, the Committee took the view that if this was advantageous for a child from a relatively privileged background, egalitarianism required that it should be a benefit shared by those less advantaged. The Longford group, like the Ingleby Committee of 1956–60,[27] considered that the differences between delinquent children and those in need of care or control were arbitrary and unreal. The Children and Young Persons Act of 1963 had disappointed reformers in that it did nothing to minimize the legal distinction and only raised the age of criminal responsibility from eight to ten years.[28] Like Ingleby, the Longford group saw the needs of children as being best met in the general context of provisions for the welfare of the family.

Accordingly, the report recommended the establishment of a Family Service with responsibility for all children and young persons up to the age of 18, pursuing a generic rather than specialist social work approach. Secondly, the juvenile court was to be absorbed into a new Family Court which would not be a criminal court; thirdly, there would be a Young Persons Court to deal with criminal matters in respect of those aged 18–21 years.

None of these proposals, to the dismay of several members of the Committee, was ever directly incorporated into government policy, but the impetus was sufficient to stimulate two

White Papers and eventually legislation in 1969. The first appeared in August 1965 entitled *The Child, the Family and the Young Offender*.[29] It might have been closer to the Longford proposals but for the fact that a Committee under Lord Kilbrandon had reported upon the need for change in Scotland.[30] Family Councils were totally to replace the juvenile courts and the age of criminal responsibility was to be set at 16 years. All children under this age would be dealt with by the councils in an informal atmosphere, away from court buildings. There would remain a Family Court to deal with dispute cases and make a finding on the evidence, but it would be for the Council to make a disposition. As in the Longford proposals, the White Paper suggested that the Family Court should deal with criminal cases from 18 to 21 years.

The White Paper was the subject of hostility and derision from its critics, the most important objection being that it heralded the diminution of the legal rights of children, not least to the benefits of 'due process'.[31] Magistrates and probation officers were equally opposed. Almost three years later, in April 1968, the government published a second White Paper, *Children in Trouble*.[32] This proposed the retention of the juvenile court, but changes in both the means of a child getting to court and the disposition of cases afterwards. Essentially, it was this White Paper which formed the basis for the Children and Young Persons Act of 1969. The Act abolished approved school orders, probation orders and what were known as 'Fit Person' orders. In their place, juvenile courts could only make supervision orders or care orders. In the case of the former, children and young persons who had left school were to be supervised by probation officers, but the younger children were to be the responsibility of local authority social workers. Similarly, the care orders were to be the responsibility of social workers, over whom the courts were to have no power whatsoever. It was to be this provision that excited most of the wrath of the juvenile court magistrates; accustomed for decades to being able to commit children to particular approved schools, they now found that if the local authority social worker considered that a child should be returned to its home, even straight after the court appearance, that was how the order would be managed. The Magistrates' Association did not cease in its criticism of this provision until a much later Conservative government made provision for the courts to make custodial care orders.

To what extent the reforms of the 1960s have been successful in respect of their declared objectives is not easy to assess. In 1964 the government had appointed a Royal Commission on the Penal System which achieved distinction only by its decision to wind itself up in 1966, admitting to the enormous and impossible nature of its task. It was followed by an Advisory Council on the Penal System which had notably better success in treating of limited topics, one of which was non-custodial penalties. Its idea of 'community service' orders bore fruit and was incorporated into the Criminal Justice Act of 1972. The Hallucinogens Sub-Committee of the Advisory Committee on Drug Dependence, set up in 1967, suggested in 1968 that the law relating to cannabis could usefully be modified; although its Chairman had been no less a person than the Baroness Wootton of Abinger it produced a public uproar and found no favour at all with James Callaghan who had replaced Roy Jenkins as Home Secretary.[33] In 1966 the government turned its attention to the courts whose business had expanded greatly since the war and appointed Lord Beeching[34] to chair a Royal Commission on Assizes and Quarter Sessions. Its report provided the basis for legislation by the Heath government of 1970–4 which established the present system of Crown Courts.[35]

In six years more changes had been enacted with regard to the criminal justice system than at any time in the present century; and few governments had been so sensitive to the need to consult a range of interested parties, not all necessarily sympathetic to the government's general intentions. In this area the Wilson administration had genuinely sensed the temper of the times and sought to channel the prevailing currents of opinion rather than to impose its own solutions (of which it had none). With regard to criminal justice and to law reform generally, the contrast in performance with the six years of the Attlee government could not have been sharper or more favourable.

Notes

1 Bevan, who had challenged Gaitskell for the leadership of the party, had died in July 1960. Gaitskell, nine years his junior, had died in January 1963, his premature death at 57 leaving the way clear for Wilson's succession.

2 Macmillan in a speech at Bedford on 20 July 1957. A Conservative poster on hoardings during the 1959 election campaign showed a young family cleaning their little Austin A30 saloon car with the caption: 'Life's good under the Conservatives; don't let Labour ruin it!'

3 The early 1960s saw the beginning of a sartorial revolution in men's clothing.

4 Kennedy was 44 at the time of his election in 1960.

5 The concept has important implications for British society in the last years of the twentieth century, among them the possibility that the balance between heavy manufacturing industry and the new 'hi-tech' and service industries has shifted irreversibly away from the former, with serious consequences for the employment prospects of the worst-educated and least skilled sections of the population.

6 There had been a major social scandal involving the prosecution and imprisonment of a number of men with important social connections in the mid-1950s. When the scandal died down the government appointed a committee under the chairmanship of Sir John Wolfenden to examine the problem (Departmental Committee on Homosexual Offences and Prostitution, *Report*, London, HMSO, 1957, Cmnd 247). Under the Criminal Justice Act 1967, homosexual acts between consenting adults in private ceased to be a criminal offence. Viscount Montgomery of Alamein, however, moved an amendment in the Lords excluding serving members of the armed services from this provision.

7 Royal Commission on Marriage and Divorce, *Report* (London, HMSO, 1956, Cmnd 9678).

8 Claud Mullins, *Marriage Failures and the Children* (London, Epworth Press, 1954).

9 See Office of Population Censuses and Surveys, *Social Trends* (London, HMSO, periodically).

10 Some firms of solicitors specializing in divorce would make arrangements for a client to spend a night at a hotel with a woman who would be remunerated for her trouble in being cited as the co-respondent. It was not unknown for the 'guilty' couple to sit up all night playing cards until the next morning when the

chambermaid (who would give evidence in court) would duly enter and find them sitting up in bed awaiting their morning tea.

11 The Mental Health Act 1959 introduced important changes, especially with regard to the policy of encouraging mental patients to enter hospital voluntarily. It marked the public legitimation of therapy for the mentally ill as superior to containment and coercion.

12 For a man who had been called to the Bar in 1913, and had been a Queen's Bench judge since 1938 his views were remarkably modern. He was 66 at the time of the trial. At the Bar he was sometimes unkindly known as unstable Stable' on account of his sometimes unpredictable and generously lenient sentencing in some criminal cases. He retired in 1968 at the age of 80, living until his 90th year.

13 'The charge is a charge that the tendency of the book is to corrupt and deprave. The charge is not that the tendency of the book is either to shock or to disgust. That is not a criminal offence. The charge is that the tendency of the book is to corrupt and deprave. Then you say; "Well, corrupt and deprave whom?" to which the answer is: those whose minds are open to such immoral influences and into whose hands a publication of this sort may fall. What, exactly, does that mean? Are we to take our literary standards as being the level of something that is suitable for the decently brought up young female aged fourteen? Or do we go even further back than that and are we to be reduced to the sort of books that one reads as a child in the nursery? The answer to that is: of course not. A mass of literature, great literature, from many angles, is wholly unsuitable for reading by the adolescent, but that does not mean that a publisher is guilty of a criminal offence for making those works available to the general public . . . the book does deal with candour, or, if you prefer it, crudity, with the realities of human love and human intercourse. There is no getting away from that, and the Crown say: "Well, that is sheer filth." Is it? It may be an error of taste to write about it. It may be a matter in which, perhaps, old fashioned people would mourn the reticence that was observed in these matters yesterday, but is it sheer filth?' ([1954] 2 All ER pp. 686–8 *et passim*).

14 Obscene Publications Act 1959, S.1(1). Lord Chief Justice Cockburn had laid down a test in common law in 1868: 'the test of obscenity is this, whether the tendency of the matter charged as obscenity is to deprave and corrupt those whose minds are open to such immoral influences, and into whose hands a publication of this sort may fall' ([1868] LR 3 QB at p. 371). Stable was clearly aware of this definition in *The Philanderer* case, and in

Lady Chatterley's Lover Mr Mervyn Griffiths Jones, for the Crown, asked the jury if this was the sort of book they would like their children's nanny to happen upon and read. (Notice how both he and Stable made reference to 'nursery' and 'nanny' as if the jury would naturally have experience of these essentially privileged domestic arrangements.)

15 'In a case like this one is perhaps permitted to reflect that nobody suggests that the Director of Public Prosecutions becomes depraved or corrupted. Counsel read the book; they do not become depraved or corrupted. Witnesses read the book; they do not become depraved or corrupted. Nobody suggests the Judge and jury become depraved or corrupted. *It is always somebody else; it is never ourselves.*' See C. H. Rolph, *The Trial of Lady Chatterley* (London, Penguin, 1961). When copies of the book finally came on sale they were sometimes treated circumspectly. At the Economist Bookshop (jointly owned by *The Economist* and the London School of Economics) copies were placed by the cash register and put in plain brown paper bags after sale. At one of W. H. Smith's wholesale warehouses senior management instructed that no women packers should handle copies of the book.

16 [1962] 3 All ER 500 and [1963] 1 QB 163.

17 *Crime: a Challenge to us All*, Report of a Labour Party Study Group on Crime and the Penal System. Chairman: The Earl of Longford, PC (London, The Labour Party, 1964). The title of the report was almost certainly suggested by the name of the Oxford student society 'Crime: a Challenge' that had been formed in 1956 to discuss penal affairs. The signatories of the final report were The Earl of Longford (Chairman), Alice Bacon, MP, Tom Driberg, MP, Xenia Field, Lord Gardiner, Trevor Gibbens, Anthony Greenwood, MP, Margaret Herbison, MP, C. R. Hewitt (C. H. Rolph), Elwyn Jones, MP, James MacColl, MP, Terence Morris, Reginald Prentice, MP, Bea Serota and John Bourne (Secretary).

18 Abolished in 1964 when the London County Council was replaced by the Greater London Council and children's services became the responsibility of the boroughs.

19 Murder (Abolition of Death Penalty) Act 1965.

20 269 HL Debs, cols 424–5, 5 August 1965. In the event, during the period 1965–8 the judges only exercised this discretion in 7 per cent of the cases in which they could have done. See Legal Research Unit, Bedford College, *Criminal Homicide in England and Wales, 1957–1968* (London, October 1969, mimeo). The judges have become no more enthusiastic in the past two decades.

21 These have been interpreted as being where the subsequent offence is unlike the original in character, e.g. if the suspended sentence had been imposed for theft but the subsequent offence was for having no excise licence on a vehicle.

22 The Magistrates' Association was by now much changed. Where it had once been moderately reformist, with the majority of magistrates eschewing membership, by the late 1960s it had become a highly respectable body to which the majority of magistrates now belonged. Confirming its standing, both the Home Office and the Lord Chancellor's Department sent observers to meetings of all its key policy committees.

23 I once enquired of a Chairman of the Association what might be done about those appointed before 1965 but who declined to take up the opportunities for training. His reply was epigrammatic and revealing: 'Where there is death, there is hope.'

24 The principal exception being borstal training from which young offenders could be released on license which could be revoked for the outstanding period of the three-year sentence. The same had applied to corrective training, which the 1967 Act abolished.

25 Hugh Klare, the Secretary of the League, showed little interest in the idea of an independent parole board, in contrast to some members of the League's executive committee.

26 One Chairman of the Parole Board admitted in a radio interview that if a man's wife were having an affair (whilst he was in prison) it might be unwise to release him lest he should be tempted to persuade the other man to desist by violent means.

27 Committee on Children and Young Persons, *Report* (London, HMSO, 1960, Cmnd 1191).

28 Originally, by the practice of the common law, it had been seven. It was raised to eight by the Children and Young Persons Act 1933.

29 London, HMSO, 1965, Cmnd 2742.

30 Committee on Children and Young Persons (Scotland), *Report* (London, HMSO, 1964, Cmnd 2306). The 'hearings' system was readily incorporated into the legal system in Scotland. See also Allison Morris, Henri Giller, Elizabeth Szwed and Hugh Geach. *Providing Criminal Justice for Children.* London, Macmillan, 1982.

31 In 1967 a case came to the Supreme Court of the United States that was to prove to be of historical significance. It arose out of an incident in 1964 which involved the question of whether a juvenile had enjoyed the benefit of 'due process'. It was fundamentally to shift the balance in the US juvenile court system back from the 'welfare' to the 'justice' model. In *re. Gault*, 387 US 1 (1967). For a very full discussion of the Gault case and the controversy over

the White Papers, see Penelope Jane Tomlinson, 'Process and Conflict in the Juvenile Court' (University of London, Ph.D. thesis, 1975 (unpublished) chapter 3).

32 London HMSO, 1968, Cmnd 3601.

33 Barbara Wootton (Baroness Wootton of Abinger), *Crime and Penal Policy: Reflections of Fifty Years Experience* (London, Allen and Unwin, 1978). She was among the most influential of the reforming voices of the time.

34 Chairman of the British Railways Board 1963–5 and probably better known for his substantial reduction of the railway network.

35 *Report* (London, HMSO, 1969, Cmnd 4153).

9 The Penal Crisis, 1960–1988

The term 'crisis' is normally taken to represent a state of affairs that is so acute as to constitute a danger; there is, however, another meaning used in relation to disease, namely the turning point at which the patient either begins to improve or sinks into a fatal decline. Although there is no single year which can be identified as the time at which things in the British prison system began to take a decided turn for the worse, change was to occur in the 1960s that has all the appearance of being irreversible.

In 1960, while the mood of the country was optimistic, in that the standard of living had never been higher and there were expectations of even better to come, among those concerned with the operation of the criminal justice system there was already a sense of foreboding. It was perfectly clear that rising living standards had not resulted in a reduction of crime but the very reverse. In practical terms, the courts were having to deal with more people, but nowhere was the problem more acutely felt than in the prison system.

Obsolete prisons and overcrowding

The prison estate[1] was, with the exceptions of Camp Hill prison on the Isle of Wight, which had been built in 1912, and Everthorpe, a strange replica of Wormwood Scrubs opened in 1957, in excess of 100 years old. Pentonville, the New Model Prison of the Victorian Convict Commissioners had opened in

1842; between then and 1860, over 50 prisons were built based on its semi-radial design.[2] Dartmoor, originally constructed to house French prisoners during the Napoleonic wars, was rebuilt in the early 1850s.[3] Wormwood Scrubs, a departure from the radial design with separate rectangular cell blocks, was opened in 1867.[4] By the early 1960s they were in relatively poor condition, many of them built of the London Stock brick that had not aged well and which needed urgent repointing. Plumbing and sanitation was generally poor and heating rudimentary.[5]

It was into these ageing prisons that the bulk of prisoners were sent by the courts.[6] The problem was not limited to the condition of prisons, in which the 'slopping out' of chamber pots was a daily routine, but that of overcrowding. From a prewar daily average of between 10,000 and 11,000, the prison population rose to a peak of 24,000 in 1952, falling back to 20,400 in 1955. But at the beginning of that year the number of prisoners sleeping three to a cell rose to 3,200 and even though it fell back to 2,400 by the end of the year that still constituted 10 per cent of the prison population.

The overcrowding was limited to local prisons, where remand prisoners, mostly untried, and short-sentence inmates were held; in the long-term prisons there was often a spare capacity. The prison population rose moderately during the late 1950s to a new peak of just over 26,000 in 1959, the year after the First Offenders Act of 1958 had come into force, severely restricting the powers of the courts to imprison offenders in this category. By 1960, the population had fallen to just under 22,000 but thereafter it began to rise, since when it has not ceased to do so. By August 1985, the population had reached the figure of just over 48,000.[7] The conditions of detention deteriorated: in the 40 years between 1946 and 1986 the prison population approximately trebled but in spite of the development of new facilities in the 1970s and 1980s the CNA (certified normal accomodation) had barely doubled.[8]

In terms of human squalor the bare statistics of multiple cell occupation tend to conceal the reality. In March 1984 11,400 inmates were being held two to a cell and 4,500 three to a cell. In local prisons this could mean prisoners being confined, complete with their beds and chamber pots, in what is a brick chamber 13 × 10 × 7 ft with a single high window of which normally no more than two panes, approximately 4½ × 4½ in, can be opened. Here, inmates can be confined for up to 18 hours each day and for longer at weekends. So bad has the squalor become that the Chief Inspector of Prisons was moved to specify details in his report for 1984.[9]

But to chart this course of progressive deterioration we need to return to the early 1960s. Although faced with increasing pressures, the Prison Commissioners (the scholarly Sir Lionel Fox having been replaced by a career civil servant, Arthur Petersen) retained the essentials of their post-war policy. Both Fox and Petersen were committed to the ideals of progressive penal reform; both were sympathetic to the aims of the Howard League and conducted a policy of openness as far as access to penal establishments by responsible observers was concerned.[10] The idea that the regimes of the prison and Borstal systems could make a positive contribution to turning offenders away from crime, by giving them skills that they lacked, improving their literacy and numeracy and providing young offenders especially with the stimulus to positive development that was lacking in their ordinary lives, was one that had both a humanitarian appeal and an intellectual credibility. Harsh penal conditions, no matter what Sir Edmund du Cane and Sir James Fitzjames Stephen might have believed in the 1880s, whatever they achieved by making prisoners' lives utterly miserable, had not secured a reduction in crime; the fall in the prison population of the 1930s had resulted from the use of enlightened alternative measures.

The relentless increase in the prison population, at a time when government was not disposed to spend money either on the prison estate or significantly on staffing or other resources created an underlying anxiety in Horseferry House, the headquarters of the Prison Commission. Individually, the Commissioners were men of great sensitivity and not a few of them, like the saintly Quaker, Duncan Fairn,[11] had had practical experience of working with offenders. They clung to their ideals which incorporated a desire eventually to *reduce* the number of establishments, as had been possible in the 1930s.

The closure of Dartmoor was in this context a symbol of their aims, and throughout the late 1950s and early 1960s the 'closure of Dartmoor' was frequently spoken of as if the event were imminent. Dartmoor, however, remains as a solid testimony to the durability of its granite construction, now well into its second century.

Change forced on by events

Two events in 1963, totally unconnected, were in their different ways to have an effect on the modern British prison system. The first was the abolition of the Prison Commission. In his report to the Home Secretary, Henry Brooke, in March 1963, Petersen notes in a brief ten words 'This will be the last Report of the Prison Commissioners.'[12] The brevity of this epitaph for one of the most outstanding of Victorian innovations which endured into the present century even longer than the Poor Law was perhaps characteristic of the 1960s which was a period that had little patience with the past, whether manifested in its architecture or its institutions. The abortive Criminal Justice Bill of 1938 had sought to abolish the Prison Commission and the proposal was revived in 1948, only to be withdrawn by Chuter Ede at the committee stage in the face of considerable opposition. The idea finally succeeded in the Criminal Justice Act 1961. The reasons for the initiative are obscure, although the Scottish Prison Commission had been abolished in 1928. Whether it was a political initiative or originated among the Civil Service mandarins is a question that only the most detailed historical research could answer.

It was widely criticized by the penal reform lobby on the grounds that it would remove those responsible for prisons from public view, permitting less public interchange on questions of penal affairs and allowing the administration of prisons to become lost in the labyrinthine passages of an anonymous bureaucracy. There is no evidence that the Commissioners themselves were particularly enthusiastic about the change, indeed they had consistently exploited their public identity to their own advantage by presenting a 'human face' of prison management.

This may not be the point at which to assess whether the past 25 years have been successful in respect of the abolition of the Commission. For while the career civil servants responsible for prisons have continued to work alongside former prison personnel absorbed into the Prison Department, it can be argued that the location of prison administration within the Home Office itself has made it easier for government ministers to impress their will upon the prison system. As we shall soon see, by the time Mountbatten came to examine the prison service one of the problems that was uppermost in his mind was that of a proper inspectorate.

Audacious crimes, escapes and the Mountbatten Report

This was the second event that had a profound effect upon the prison system. The events leading up to the inquiry go back to 1962. In March 1962, George Blake, who had been working as a double agent for both M16 and the KGB,[13] was convicted of espionage and sentenced to 42 years' imprisonment. It was the longest fixed-term sentence ever imposed in an English criminal court, and Blake was taken away to serve his time in Wormwood Scrubs along with the growing number of long-term prisoners, the Homicide Act of 1957 having caused an increase in the mandatory life sentence population. Then, in August 1963, there took place the most audacious robbery in the annals of British crime: a group of men by dint of immensely careful planning held up a mail train carrying some £250,000 in old ten shilling (50 pence in modern money) banknotes by stopping it at a red signal. Until then, the largest sum ever taken in a robbery was that stolen from a Post Office van in Eastcastle Street in the West End of London in 1952 when £30,000 had been taken. But whereas the Eastcastle Street gang were never caught, the fate of the Great Train Robbers was more dismal. One by one they were taken and, when convicted, received sentences varying between 25 and 30 years. George Blake notwithstanding, these were regarded as sentences of astonishing severity, but the prison authorities took matters in their stride and duly distributed them around various closed prisons throughout the country. One, however, decided not to remain even for part of the 20 years which he would have had to serve with one-third remission for good conduct and absconded from Winson Green prison in Birmingham. That he could do so with apparent ease cast serious doubts on prison security, for the system then was for surveillance during the night hours to be in the hands of a rudimentary night watch. The Prison Department managed successfully to avoid a public inquiry and the incident would have been forgotten but for the fact that the following year a second train robber, Ronald Biggs, destined to become the most famous escaped felon since Jack Sheppard broke out of Newgate in the reign of George II, made good his escape from Wandsworth in broad daylight by the simple expedient of having his friends drive a furniture pantechnicon up to the wall of the prison by the exercise yard. A rope was thrown over with a ladder and Biggs and another man (later recaptured) scaled the wall and climbed into the furniture van by means of a hatch that had been cut in its roof.[14] This time the outcry was somewhat louder, no doubt on account of the audacity of the method employed but the Prison Department was not greatly moved. Fairn, who was directly responsible (he had been Chief Director on the Prisons Board), was privately warned by his friends that unless the Department was seen to be taking a less cavalier attitude serious political trouble would soon be brewing.[15] Matters came to a head in November 1966 when George Blake, having served only four of his 42 years, escaped from Wormwood Scrubs. The physical effort required to break out of 'D' Hall had not been very great; the brickwork around a window was in such poor condition that he had been able to kick a hole in it with his prison footwear.

This time there was no chance of either the Department or indeed the government itself escaping censure. Roy Jenkins, who had succeeded Sir Frank Soskice at the Home Office less than a year before, was quick to recognize the danger.[16] It was not that the public was so much concerned with prison escapes as it was with spies, and from the late 1950s there had been a series of cases involving spies and double agents – Burgess, MacLean, Philby, Houghton, Gee, Vassal and Bossard.[17] Jenkins's period at the Home Office was characterized by both a commitment to liberal penal values and a realistic assessment of how far one could be casual about what might be the making of a political crisis.[18] His reaction was to invite Admiral of the

Fleet, Earl Mountbatten of Burma, to conduct a brief but searching inquiry into the escape of Blake and prison security generally. It was an astute move for Mountbatten was not only a senior member of the Royal Family but also a man held in the highest public regard as a war hero.[19] He had been last Viceroy of India and subsequently Chief of the Defence Staff.

Mountbatten, for his part, made it clear to Jenkins that he was only prepared to undertake the task on the condition that if he made recommendations they would be acted upon; he was not prepared to waste his time.[20]

Mountbatten's investigation was remarkable, not merely for the speed with which it was conducted, but the degree of insight he was able to develop into the arcane practice of prison administration.[21] The escapes he showed to be the result of inadequate techniques of surveillance and he made a number of recommendations that were to have far-reaching significance. He also recognized that management structures were not all that they might be and made some pertinent suggestions in that direction.

Mountbatten took the view that there ought to be a fourfold security classification of inmates. Category A were to be the highest risk for whom escape was to be made to all intents and purposes impossible. Category B were those whose escape would not be a threat to national security or constitute a major public danger, but those for whom escape, nevertheless, must be made extremely difficult. Category C were those inmates who could not be trusted with open conditions, but who would not be highly motivated to escape and who did not constitute the kind of threat posed by those in categories A and B. Category D prisoners were those who could be safely accommodated in open establishments.

The problem then arose as to where the category A men were to be accommodated. Mountbatten had no doubts. A new prison was then in the course of construction at Albany on the Isle of Wight, close to the existing long-term maximum security prison of Parkhurst (completed *c.*1840) and the training prison at Camp Hill (1912). Mountbatten, who happened also to be Governor of the Isle of Wight, considered that this was the ideal place and even suggested a name, 'Vectis', the Roman name for the island but also that of the local bus company who were not enthusiastic at the choice. He considered that probably not more than 250–300 prisoners would fall into category A and that they could all be comfortably accommodated in this island prison which, in addition to electronic security (including equipment to sense movement across the ground beneath the walls), would have the final cordon of the fierce tidal waters of the Solent and the English Channel.

Reactions within the Prison Department to the idea of a British Alcatraz were distinctly unenthusiastic, but no more than to one of his other proposals – that of the appointment of an Inspector General of Prisons who would have direct access to the Secretary of State, bypassing both the Director of Prison Administration and the Permanent Under-Secretary at the Home Office. His suggestion that there was an insufficient grading of ranks within the prison service and that a new rank of senior officer should be created between the basic grade of prison officer and that of principal officer was, in contrast, accepted without ado.

What the Mountbatten proposals implied was the biggest administrative change in the prison system since the establishment of the Prison Commission in 1877. Never before had there been such a precise classification of inmates in terms of security risk and never, even in the days of the convict prisons, had there been a proposal to allocate the most serious risks to a particular place. The implications for the prison development programme were fundamental. But prison administration apart, the notion that an Inspector General should be able to go over the heads of the most senior permanent officials was seen as unacceptable. The Prison Commission, which had had the duty of reporting direct to the Home Secretary had only just been abolished and Mountbatten's proposal ran directly counter to the policy that had been implemented five years previously which had reduced the autonomy of the prison system by bringing it into the Home Office. In the event, Mountbatten's nominee was appointed, but things did not work out quite as Mountbatten had intended.[22] The Home Office view of events and that of Mountbatten subsequently differed. He came to the conclusion that the permanent officials had been determined to thwart his proposals from the outset, while they took the view that they did nothing of the sort. It will be for a future historian of the prison service to strike some balance between these two opposing accounts of what actually happened.[23] What eventually transpired was the establishment of a Prisons Inspectorate which, had Mountbatten lived to see its development and robust pronouncements in the 1980s, would no doubt have given him a sense of satisfaction.

More important was the fate of Mountbatten's proposals regarding security. As far as the classification into categories of risk was concerned, the task began almost immediately, but the issue of a special maximum security prison to accommodate category A inmates was altogether more vexed. So far, the only specialist institution to have been built was the psychiatric prison at Grendon Underwood which opened in 1962, though to some extent the hospital wing at Parkhurst had been functioning as a geriatric unit for some years.

Concentration versus dispersal

Shortly before Mountbatten reported in December 1966 a sub-committee of the House of Commons Estimates Committee on Social Affairs began an inquiry into prisons, including the topic of security, and it reported in August 1967. But the specific question of what to do about Mountbatten's proposals for classification was more urgent. In the short run, the Prison Department began to invest in rolls of barbed wire hastily set on prison walls, floodlighting and the purchase of Alsatian dogs, but the long-term issue was entrusted in February 1967 to the Advisory Council on the Penal System. It in turn set up a sub-committee under the Chairmanship of Leon Radzinowicz, Wolfson Professor of Criminology in the University of Cambridge.

When it reported in March 1968 it categorically rejected the 'concentration' solution of Mountbatten's 'Vectis' and recommended the dispersal of category A prisoners into four separate institutions. This was undoubtedly the preferred solution of the Home Office which was concerned not only with the prospect of how to organize a regime for prisoners all of whom presented potential problems of intractibility but with the cost of adapting the design of Albany for the purpose.

Supporters of the Mountbatten proposal considered that the Home Office had made its wishes abundantly clear to the Radzinowicz Committee in advance, though whether the Home Office would have gone ahead if the Committee had recommended in favour of concentration is by no means certain.

What is certain is that the dispersal policy contained within it the seeds of future difficulties. For whereas the limitation of category A to a single prison would have put a constraint on numbers, dispersal offered no such safeguard. Moreover, as dispersal developed, so it became the case that the standards of security became geared to the requirements of category A rather than the majority of category B inmates. And as far as disruptive influences were concerned, the presence of category A men in an increasing number of closed prisons meant that the problems of security and discipline were enlarged as well as dispersed as prison disorders in the 1970s were to demonstrate. Nor was the problem confined to category A prisons; from the end of 1967 any prison that contained category B prisoners, even if the majority were classified as C, began to manifest the characteristics of security appropriate to the highest category of inmate irrespective of their relative numbers in the population. When prisons like Pentonville, which by 1967 had been dedicated to holding recidivists serving less than 12 months, became be-decked with wire, closed-circuit TV cameras, dogs and all the other *impedimenta* of security, cynics remarked that the inhabitants of Islington could sleep safe in their beds in the knowledge that the prison's pathetic collection of drunks and vagrants serving short sentences were safely contained within its walls.

Mountbatten vilified

The imposition of the new security regimes had the effect of limiting freedom of movement within the prison buildings, in consequence of which the liberal and constructive programmes patiently built up over a period of 20 years were seriously eroded. Educational classes and hobby groups were among the first to suffer. The allotment gardens that Gilbert Hair had organized for the lifers at Wormwood Scrubs disappeared under the 'dog track' of the steel-mesh inner perimeter fence.[25] Prison reformers, voluntary workers in prisons, those who came in to teach evening classes and prison visitors began to complain at the changes. All too readily the prison authorities laid the blame at the door of the Mountbatten Report for which Mountbatten was held personally responsible.

Mountbatten himself became deeply disturbed at these criticisms. What he had intended was that under conditions of increased perimeter security there should be a regime of 'humane containment', even in 'Vectis'. The last thing he had envisaged was for high-security prisoners to move about a prison, being signed for as they passed from one place to another as if they were objects rather than people. As a member of the Royal Family, he considered himself precluded from making a speech in the House of Lords to correct what he believed to be a gross distortion of his views; instead, he used his connections in the liberal 'establishment' that in the late 1960s hung like a corona about the Wilsonian epicentre to disseminate his side of the story. History will almost certainly acquit him of any bad faith.

A new prison building programme

Both pressure of numbers and the demands of the new classification arrangements made it imperative for the Home Office to examine the future of the prison system, not least with respect to its building programme. Towards the end of 1969 the White Paper, *People in Prison*, appeared.[26] As Richard Sparks wrote, almost prophetically, in 1971:

> *People in Prison* may also mark the end, in England, of the whole penological era which began with the publication of the Gladstone report in 1895. A major objective of penal policy during that time . . . has been to keep as many offenders as possible out of prison. But it is possible, even likely, that this objective is no longer realistic.[27]

Sparks also accurately predicted that the prison population would rise and that the increase would be largely confined to the local prisons. He wrote: 'Plainly some action is imperative, in the near future, if a large part of the English prison system is to be prevented from returning to something like the condition in which John Howard found it.'[28]

What the White Paper did was to sketch out a new strategy in which it was assumed that the prison population would rise; consequently, there was a need for a new prison building programme. But what the programme was to provide was not a respite for the increasingly overcrowded and antiquated local prisons whose through-put of prisoners would be greatest and where overcrowding would be most keenly felt, but an expansion of those establishments able to take more long- and medium-term prisoners. And in the 1960s with the sentences on spies and train robbers, the High Court judges seemed to be setting new definitions of what was a long sentence. Back in 1948 a ten-year sentence had been considered long, but with 30 years for train robbers and 25 years for gangland criminals, long sentences in the late 1960s and early 1970s had increased by 50 per cent or more, influenced in the opinion of some, by the existence of a parole system.

By 1975 it had become evident that some review of sentencing was becoming urgent, and Roy Jenkins asked the Advisory Council on the Penal System to conduct a review of maximum penalties of imprisonment. Once more, the Council conducted a scholarly inquiry reporting in February 1978 to Jenkins's successor, Merlyn Rees.[29] The Council, which comprised a number of distinguished experts and included senior members of the judiciary, made some suggestions for reduction which were highly controversial, including reducing the legal *maxima* to accord with the actual pattern of sentencing.[30]

Declining morale

The fears of Sparks were realized by the mid-1970s, but worse was to befall. The prison service, once characterized by a high level of morale and discipline from the governor grades down, many of those in the uniformed grades being long engagement regular ex-servicemen, began to experience serious industrial disputes. The causes of the troubles were complex and, although they were focused on discontent about pay, allowances and conditions, there is good reason to believe that after the fundamental shift in philosophy following the implementation of the Home Office interpretation of the Mountbatten report, the basic grades of prison staff became progressively more demoralized as the constructive elements in their roles seemed to diminish. Increasingly they devoted their energies not to rehabilitation but containment.[31] As the conditions in prison became more squalid, so the working conditions of prison staff became more disagreeable.

There were 'walk outs', periods of 'working to rule' and, probably most disruptive of all, working to rule in the production of prisoners for trial.[32] The law officers of the Crown were extremely cautious and eschewed any prosecution of individual prison officers for the wilful obstruction of justice, leaving judges and magistrates to contain what became their increasingly impotent fury.[33] Meanwhile, the prison population continued to grow. In November 1978, Merlyn Rees set up an inquiry under the Chairmanship of Mr Justice May to inquire into the state of the United Kingdom prison services. It was significant that the inquiry was to include Scotland and the Province of Northern Ireland, since the industrial troubles had spread beyond England and Wales. Rees had hoped that the Committee would take only a brief time and report in March 1979, but the Committee had to make it clear to him that on account of the wide terms of reference March was an impossible date. In February, Rees told the Commons that it was hoped to have a report in the summer.[34] In the event it did not appear until October, by which time the Thatcher administration had been in office for some five months.

Prisons enter the Thatcher era

The difficulty with an inquiry set up by one government but reporting to another is that its final handiwork may take on the character of an 'unwanted gift'. It is highly doubtful whether, had the Conservatives been in office during the worst of the trouble, the government would even have considered the establishment of the May Committee or anything like it; since 1979, its style has been to seek the assistance of high-powered individuals from the world of commerce to conduct managerial-style reviews. Certainly nothing like the painstaking work of the May inquiry has been discernible in, say, inquiries into aspects of health care. That the Advisory Council on the Penal System was abolished provides a further indication that since 1979 the style of the government, as far as the criminal justice system is concerned, has fundamentally changed.

Rees's successor at the Home Office was William Whitelaw. In an important sense Whitelaw's tenure of office marked the conclusion of an era that had begun in 1945 in that he was the last of a line of Home Secretaries who, although some were unpopular in their time, seldom sought to generate a high political profile for their work in the criminal justice field and never departed from the practice, established since Victorian times, of calling upon volunteers from among the 'great and the good' to serve on advisory bodies.

Whitelaw, however, had to deal with a party flushed with victory that was unlike the Conservative party of his youth. It was newly self-confident and consciously contemptuous of the 'post-war settlement'. In consequence, when Whitelaw appeared at the party conferences he was regularly given a hostile reception, unsubtly suggesting that he was not one of the ministers of the new administration who was 'delivering'. His successor, Leon Brittan, who had been his junior colleague at the Home Office in 1979 (followed by a spell at the Treasury) had an entirely different approach. At the party conference in October 1983 he announced restrictive new regulations governing parole for certain classes of 'serious' offenders, precipitating a protracted law suit in the process.[35] In May 1984 the Home Office published *Criminal Justice: A Working Paper* with a Foreword by the Home Secretary.[36] In content and tone, it reads less like a 'working paper' and more like a political pamphlet, setting out the government's intentions regarding the control of crime in general, the police and a prison-building programme.

In his speech to the Conservative Party Conference in Blackpool on 11 October 1983 Brittan had told the delegates: 'I am . . . glad to say that the measures I have outlined today will put us on course for ending prison overcrowding by the end of the decade.' In November 1986 the Working Paper appeared in a revised edition under the signature of Douglas Hurd who had replaced Brittan at the Home Office. Although in the nature of a progress report, the second edition is significantly lacking in any statement of expectation about overcrowding ceasing by the end of the decade.

The trend of prison population has been otherwise. In 1984 the Home Office projection envisaged a daily average population of 46,000 in 1989 rising to 48,700 in 1990 and 49,600 in 1991,[37] but by July 1985 the figure had reached 48,037. Although the numbers fell back during 1986, prison conditions worsened. The practice of holding prisoners in police cells that had begun in 1983 – and was briefly discontinued for less than a month – had become an established practice. The average each day was now only about 70 men and 40 women, compared with a total average in 1983 of 280. These prisoners were – and are – being held in accommodation that was – and is – substantially poorer than that provided in prison.[38]

The number of inmates from ethnic minorities has grown substantially in recent years. In 1959 the population of Pentonville contained barely 4 per cent from the ethnic minorities.[39] By 1985, 12.5 per cent of men and 17 per cent of women in penal institutions were from ethnic minorities; among the remand population of untried or unsentenced prisoners they constituted 16 per cent of men and 23 per cent of women. Among adult males sentenced to periods in excess of four years 18 per cent were from minority groups.

None of this can be taken as an indication that ethnicity *per se* has anything to do with a propensity to commit crime. Rather, it has to be understood in terms of the individual's socioeconomic status. In nineteeth-century England, the Irish were a disproportionate section of the prison population and in the United States, the Irish, the Italians and currently the blacks and Hispanics have at various times constituted a disproportionate part of the total. As the status of groups improves, so the propensity to become involved in crime and be imprisoned diminishes. Once in prison, however, racial issues assume new dimensions of importance, and although such evidence as there is suggests that discrimination is not widespread it represents a potentially volatile feature within a system that is already fraught with difficulties.

There are now two schools of thought about prisons. One was reflected in the thinking of the May report and to some degree in the government's own thinking, namely everything possible must be done to reduce the potential prison population, but adequate provision must be made to deal with the continuing problem of overcrowding. The other is more uncompromising and takes the view that populations of institutions expand to fill new space as it becomes available. Hence there should be an end to expanding the prison system, new building merely replacing the old. Certainly, there is no evidence that even now that there are 124 penal establishments and more on the way, overcrowding has been ameliorated since the flow from the courts does not diminish. There is, perhaps, a further phase in the history of imprisonment in Britain that is yet to come; one in which imprisonment will be, as far as the courts are concerned, a rare event, reserved only for those whose continued liberty in the community constitutes a danger to the physical well-being of others. For all other offenders, including those now imprisoned, it is possible that new and more ingenious options may be found.

Notes

1 The term used to describe the stock of prison buildings.
2 See Terence Morris, Pauline Morris and Barbara Barer, *Pentonville: the Sociology of an English Prison* (London, Routledge and Kegan Paul, 1963).
3 The original gateway from its prisoner of war days still stands with the inscription *parcere subjectis* (pity the conquered).
4 Built to the designs of Sir Edmund Du Cane the entrance façade incorporates large bas-reliefs of the pioneer penal reformers John Howard and Elizabeth Fry.
5 In the winter of 1955–6, I sat with a prisoner in his cell in 'D' hall of Wormwood Scrubs. It was about 8 o'clock in the evening and the water in the prisoner's enamel jug had a thin sheet of ice on it.
6 The relatively small number of 'open' prisons were used mainly for 'white collar' offenders and those long-sentence men of good behaviour who were nearing release.
7 Statistics for prison populations are derived from the annual

reports of the Prison Commissioners up to that for the year 1962 (Cmnd 2030, 1963) and thereafter from *Reports of the Work of the Prison Department* (annually).

8 Home Office, *Criminal Justice: a Working Paper* (London, HMSO, 1984, rev. edn 1986).

9 On the night of 30 August 1984, of a population of some 42,000 over a quarter 'were locked in a cell on their own and had to use chamber pots when they wished to urinate or defaecate; over a third had to use chamber pots while sharing a cell (or occasionally in a dormitory) with one or more inmates; about a ninth were in accommodation with integral sanitation; about a quarter were in accommodation which allowed them access to communal toilets . . . When the time for slopping out comes the prisoners queue up with their pots for the few toilets on the landing. The stench of urine and excrement pervades the prison. So awful is this procedure that many prisoners become constipated – others prefer to use their pants, hurling them and their contents out of the window when morning comes' (*Report of Her Majesty's Chief Inspector of Prisons*, London, HMSO, 1984).

10 It was Fox who authorized the first prison researches at Bristol prison and later at Maidstone and Pentonville. See Morris, Morris and Barer, *Pentonville.* Without the personal support of Petersen, it is unlikely that the Home Office would have permitted publication of the final draft of the Pentonville book which was felt by some to be too close to the bone in its account of prison life. The Governor of Pentonville, David Waddilove, had given the research his wholehearted support.

11 Fairn, who had joined the prison service in the Borstal section in the early 1930s had been Governor of Oxford prison. He visited and corresponded with individual prisoners long after his retirement. Cape, who was responsible for education, had been a housemaster at the time of the famous march from Feltham to the new open Borstal at Lowdham Grange. See Terence Morris, 'British criminology 1935–48', *British Journal of Criminology* (1988), 28, pp. 22–34.

12 *Report of the Commissioners of Prisons for the Year 1962* (London, HMSO, 1963, Cmnd 2030). A summary of the events surrounding the abolition of the Prison Commission can be found in the *Report of the Committee of Inquiry into the United Kingdom Prison Services* (London, HMSO, 1979, Cmnd 7673, The May Report).

13 Details of Blake's activities are given in Peter Wright, *Spycatcher* (New York, Viking Penguin, 1987).

14 Biggs is still at liberty in Brazil, the only one of the train robbers

who has not had to complete his sentence. For an account of the robbery, see Peta Fordham, *The Robbers' Tale* (London, Hodder and Stoughton, 1965).

15 Conversations between Fairn and myself during 1965 and 1966.

16 Soskice had been appointed by Wilson in 1964 but he was a sick man and made no mark upon penal affairs nor on the Home Office generally.

17 Vassal had been sentenced to 18 years in 1959 and Bossard to 25 years in May 1965.

18 At the 1964 election Labour had secured an overall majority of four seats; this was increased to 96 at the election of 1966.

19 For those who had served under Mountbatten, especially at sea and in the ill-fated destroyer *Kelly*, he was the object of immense personal affection.

20 Conversations between Mountbatten and myself in 1968.

21 *Report of the Inquiry into Prison Escapes and Security* (London, HMSO, 1966, Cmnd 3175).

22 Mountbatten had recommended the name of Brigadier Maunsell who had been on his staff in Combined Operations in the Far East. He described Maunsell as a 'brilliant officer' (personal conversation).

23 Conversations between Mountbatten and myself and subsequent correspondence between myself and a former senior permanent official at the Home Office.

24 Advisory Council on the Penal System, *The Regime for Long Term Prisoners in Conditions of Maximum Security* (HMSO, 1968).

25 Hair, who had been an enlightened governor of both Strangeways in Manchester and Wormwood Scrubs became an Assistant Commissioner in 1961. In the first film ever to be made inside a British prison (at Strangeways in 1956) he described the work of the prison service as being rather like that in the Post Office which deals with damaged parcels. 'It's our job to put these human parcels together again as best we can.' It was a noble conception, if naïvely expressed. *In Prison*, a film for BBC television made by Denis Mitchell.

26 London, HMSO, 1969, Cmnd 4214.

27 Richard Sparks, *Local Prisons: the Crisis in the English Penal System* (London, Heinemann, 1971).

28 Sparks, *Local Prisons*, p. 91.

29 Advisory Council on the Penal System, *Sentences of Imprisonment: a Review of Maximum Penalties* (London, HMSO, 1978). It was to prove the last major work of the Advisory Council which was abolished by the first Thatcher administration in 1979.

30 'For the ordinary offender, new maximum penalties should be fixed at the level below which 90% of sentences of immediate imprisonment passed by the Crown Court for the particular offence have fallen in recent years' (Advisory Council on the Penal System, *Sentences of Imprisonment*, para. 20).

31 The evidence of the Prison Officers' Association to the Wynn Parry Committee had included a stress on the constructive and rehabilitative task of the ordinary prison officer, *Remuneration and Conditions of Service of Certain Grades in the Prison Service* (London, HMSO, 1958, Cmnd 544).

32 One Crown Court was paralysed for over a week because prisoners were not produced for trial until late in the day, leaving judges and juries sitting idle.

33 This was the period in which the Callaghan government became increasingly ineffective in controlling trade union militancy.

34 HC Debs, cols 182–3, 21 February 1979.

35 *In re. Findlay and Others* [1984] 3 WLR. The Chairman of the Parole Board refers to this case in David Windlesham, *Responses to Crime* (Oxford, The Clarendon Press, 1987). For a more critical view of the matter, see Terence Morris, 'Is Brittan's justice still best?', *New Society*, 7 March 1983.

36 London, HMSO, 1984.

37 Home Office. 'Projections of Long Term Trends in the Prison Population to 1993' (Home Office Statistical Bulletin, no. 15, 1985).

38 In the police cells under some of the new London Magistrates' Courts there is access to neither natural daylight nor fresh air. In December 1988 it was again announced that no prisoners were being held in police cells instead of prison. How long this will continue may be sceptically viewed in the light of previons experience.

39 Morris, Morris and Barer, *Pentonville*, pp. 60–1.

10 The New Policing

The organization of policing was importantly affected by the Police Act of 1964, following upon the work of the Royal Commission of 1962.[1] But in examining the period since the 1964 Act it is impossible to discount the effect of political and social events occurring as the natural phenomena to which the police service has had to respond. In such interactive situations, neither the police nor the participants concerned operate independently; just as police responses are affected by immediate past experience so, too, public expectations and behaviour towards the police are modified by perceptions of police behaviour.

The Challenor scandal

The 1964 Act had not reached the statute book before the Metropolitan Police were again facing a serious allegation of impropriety. In July 1963, Queen Frederika of Greece, a distinctly unpopular figure on account of her role in Greek politics, arrived in London and proceeded to Claridges Hotel where a crowd had gathered outside. In the course of the demonstration, in which little worse happened than for the crowd to chant 'Go home, Frederika!', a number of arrests were made.[2] One was a young man, Donald Roum, who was charged with being in possession of an offensive weapon, namely a half-brick. The arresting officer was Detective Sergeant Harold Gordon Challenor who was outside Claridges on his own initiative.

Unfortunately for Challenor, Roum's solicitor had the forethought to bring him a change of clothing to the police station where he was detained; that which he had been wearing was then taken away for private forensic analysis. Bricks are made of friable material and it would be impossible to carry part of one in a pocket without traces of dust remaining; no such traces were found in Roum's jacket. In February 1964, after papers had been sent to the Director of Public Prosecutions, Challenor and three constables at Saville Row police station were put on trial.

It was clear that Roum had been 'fitted up' and that Challenor had been the *fons et origo* of the whole shabby episode, but then events took an extraordinary turn. Challenor was found to be suffering from a severe mental illness, sufficiently acute for the court to be persuaded that he was unfit to plead. Challenor departed from the court to a mental hospital but the three young constables were not so fortunate, being convicted, imprisoned and dismissed from the police service. By May, ten other cases involving 29 complaints against Challenor and other officers were investigated and, though not the subject of proceedings, settlements were made out of court.

The question which was now asked was how, if Challenor was mentally ill, no one had noticed it before. Within a month of the new Police Act coming into operation, Henry Brooke had set up the first inquiry under S.32 requesting Mr A. E. James, QC, to 'consider the circumstances in which it was possible for Sergeant Harold Gordon Challenor to continue on duty when he appeared to have been affected by the onset of mental illness'. In his report, James exonerated both the police and its medical officers of any blame and dismissed allegations of corruption as unfounded and largely actuated by malice.[3]

Demonstrations and disputes

By the late 1960s the police were having to deal with a phenomenon that had been largely quiescent for a generation: large political demonstrations. Initially, these were of a peaceful variety and even the massive 'sit down' protests of the CND Committee of 100 involved no physical violence. But 1968 was to prove a turning point. All over Western Europe students were protesting at the continuation of the American war in Vietnam and in May of that year a number of universities were forcibly occupied.[4] The police for the most part declined to enter university premises and the college authorities had to resort to the snail-like processes of the civil law to regain possession.

At the two massive demonstrations outside the United States Embassy in Grosvenor Square, however, things were very different. On the first occasion tens of thousands of protesters beseiged the embassy and it was only with the greatest difficulty that the police were able to prevent it being stormed. Scenes of disorganized hand-to-hand combat were filmed by television camera crews, the film subsequently proving to be of immense value to the police in training for public order control. Apart from indicating the unusual degree of aggression in the crowd, the film footage indicated how unprepared were the police, both in terms of the tactics employed and the command structure. Large numbers of constables sustained injuries, some of them serious. Headgear proved totally inadequate, and mounted officers were particularly vulnerable to attack when surrounded by the crowd. At the second Grosvenor Square demonstration, the police were better prepared, maintaining a defensive cordon, holding mounted officers in reserve and experimenting with 'snatch squads' to take out obvious leaders.[5]

In June 1974 the Metropolitan Police were again involved in another violent confrontation. The National Front was holding a meeting at premises in Red Lion Square in Holborn and a large number of left-wing demonstrators filled the square in an attempt to prevent the meeting taking place. This time the police were confronted with the problem of separating the two factions, but were no better equipped than they had been in 1968.[6] On this occasion the most serious outcome was the death of a young man, Kevin Gately, who happened to be in the crowd. Lord Justice Scarman was invited to conduct an inquiry and reported in 1975.[7]

Earlier in 1974 the police in the West Midlands were confronted by a major problem of public order outside the gates of the Saltley coking plant. In the course of the miners' strike in February that year (which precipitated the fall of the Heath government) a number of 'flying pickets' as they had become known, blocked the gates of the plant.[8] The West Midlands police, much less experienced than their Metropolitan colleagues, were overwhelmed and rendered impotent. It was a defeat that rankled throughout the police service and was certainly not forgotten a decade later when again outside a coking plant, this time at Orgreave, the confrontation of police and pickets was to have a very different outcome.

Industrial disputes returned to the headlines in 1977 when a dispute at the Grunwick film processing plant in north London, involving the attempt of some women workers to organize a union, resulted in a mass picket. This was in every sense a traditional trade dispute in which the employer attempted to secure the presence of the non-striking part of his workforce by bringing them in by bus and the strikers, for their part, attempting to prevent it. Large numbers of police were deployed over a considerable period, the inevitable consequence of which was to create the impression that the police were the allies of the employer. The Grunwick dispute achieved nothing in terms of industrial relations and served only to damage the public image both of trade unions and of the police. For while Conservative supporters were for the most part delighted to see trade unionists (whom they perceived as the 'overmighty subjects' who challenged the law) being successfully resisted, many Labour supporters who had no less an interest in public tranquillity were concerned at what they saw to be a growing anti-trade union bias in police activity.[9]

The 'politicization' of the police can be said to date from this period and it was to influence the public evaluation of police performance from the mid-1970s until the present. To be strictly accurate, it is not the police who have been politicized, but public attitudes towards them for, with one notable exception,[10] Chief Constables have generally been careful to eschew public pronouncements of a controversial nature. If anything, they have chosen to go their own way, determined to maintain a robust independence in operational matters.

The Metropolitan Police returned to the headlines in April 1979, once more as a consequence of activities by right-wing activists, this time in Southall, a district of West London with a large Asian population. Again, as at Red Lion Square, left-wing activists re-enacted the responses of their forebears in the 1930s and confronted the hooligans of the far right. The events at Southall were to prove disastrous for the police in more senses than one. At first there was an attempt to contain the trouble by the use of ordinary constables; they came very close to being overwhelmed by the violence which began to be directed against them. Then, after some hours and as the line was about to break, units of the new Special Patrol Group were deployed.[11] The evidence suggests that individual units were to some extent able to operate fairly independently. At the end of the day, the rioting on the streets had been quelled, but a young New Zealand schoolteacher, Blair Peach, lay dying from serious head injuries.

It has never been suggested that Peach met his death by accident in the ordinary sense of the word. What is about as certain as anything can be in such situations is that he met his death violently and unlawfully at the hands of a person or persons unknown. There was no official inquiry, as there had been into the death of Kevin Gately in Red Lion Square. The incident occurred only weeks before the General Election in May and the newly elected government of Margaret Thatcher was anxious to manifest its support for the police since 'law and order' had been an important theme in its electoral strategy. The Metropolitan Police, to the concern of some senior officers in New Scotland Yard, closed its collective ranks to the suggestion that was canvassed, not only in left-wing but in liberal circles generally, that he had died at the hands of one or more members of a unit of the Special Patrol Group. His death was investigated by the National Council for Civil Liberties, which appointed a group of highly respected individuals from the academic and legal professions to hear evidence.[12] Such evidence as came to light was, in the least, disturbing, suggesting that there had been a failure of control within the total operation. Allegations that 'unauthorized equipment' in the form of a piece of plastic hose filled with lead shot had been found in the locker of one member of a particular SPG unit became public property. (At the inquest on Peach, the pathological evidence indicated that the head injuries were of the type that *could* have been sustained from an object with a relatively soft exterior but a dense core.)

In July 1988 the Metropolitan Police paid into court a sum of £75,005 at the end of a bitter eight year battle by the Peach family. Additionally, the police agreed to pay the family's legal costs estimated at around £50,000. This offer was made with the usual qualification that it implied no admission of liability, and so, in strict legal terms it did. But the size of the payment and the acceptance of costs reflects what might well have been the outcome had the matter finally gone to a successful civil trial of the action. Peach's mother, who had initiated proceedings, died in 1983, but the case was taken up by his two brothers in New Zealand. The story does not reflect well upon the Metropolitan Police which was initially highly defensive and at times unco-operative. Perhaps the most significant aspect of the Peach case was that it reflected the inadequacies of the procedures for investigating complaints against the police. Throughout the 1980s there have been numerous cases involving many police forces in which complainants have been able to win substantial damages against the police in the civil courts or in out of court settlements, but in which the offending police officers have been subject to no internal disciplinary proceedings.

There was, however, a change in the climate within the Met. In 1986 a group of youths making their way home along the Holloway Road suddenly found themselves being assaulted by a group of men who had decanted from what appeared to be a police van. Initially none of their assailants could be identified because of the problem of establishing from which, of the several police vans in the area, they might have come. Innocent police officers rightly denied their involvement in the incident. Eventually it became possible for a prosecution to be mounted and five officers were subsequently imprisoned.

In vulgar political terms after the death of Blair Peach the police were uncritically castigated as murderers and the enthusiastic supporters of racism. The reality was somewhat different. For although there was undoubtedly a degree of racism in the Metropolitan Police in the lower ranks, many of its senior officers were troubled at the way in which the operational control of public disorders was still defective. The 'Met' had to preserve a public image, but at the same time there were many in New Scotland Yard who recognized that the writing could well be on the wall as far as public tolerance of the conduct of policing was concerned. For these were not the ex-army officers who had risen to senior rank in previous generations, but policemen who had been exposed to a diversity of educational influences and who were only too aware of the social and political dimensions of policing. More important, many of those who were of senior rank in the 'Met' in the 1970s were to become the Chief and Assistant Chief Constables of other forces in the 1980s.

Drugs and pornography: problems of corruption

Although other forces had their share of trouble, it was the 'Met' that had to endure a high public profile in the 1970s. In 1973 there was a major scandal involving the Drug Squad, no less embarrassing because it involved a conflict between the Metropolitan Police and the Department of Customs and Excise. In September that year six officers went on trial charged with conspiracy to pervert the course of justice of whom five were also charged with perjury. Although all six were acquitted on the first charge, three were convicted on the second and sent to prison. Worse was to come. In February 1976 proceedings began against no fewer than 12 serving or recently retired Metropolitan officers charged with offences of corruption in their dealings with Soho pornographers. They included two ex-Commanders, one ex-Detective Chief Superintendent, four Detective Inspectors, two ex-Detective Inspectors and two ex-Detective Constables. It was the biggest trial involving detectives seen in London since 1877.[13] This was not to be the last allegation of major corruption for in the same year another investigation began under the name 'Operation Countryman'. In the event, although it continued for some five years, it was to be a mountain that laboured and brought forth a mouse. A Detective Chief Inspector and a Detective Inspector of the City of London police were convicted of conspiracy and eight Metropolitan detectives were prosecuted, all of whom were acquitted. Three were subsequently dismissed following disciplinary proceedings, one resigned and four went back on duty.[14]

Government and police after 1979

Such were the problems of the 1970s. Public confidence in the police had been shaken probably less by events involving public disorder, and the deaths of Kevin Gately and Blair Peach, than by allegations of corruption for this was a decade that was marked by allegations of corruption in public life.

The return of a Conservative government in May 1979 was to mark the most fundamental change in British politics in the present century. For the Thatcherite conception of the role of the state is distinct from anything that has gone before under the name of Conservative and in this its expectations about the role of the police have been clear and unambiguous. But these have been expressed incidentally and instrumentally rather than abstractly as the events of the first five years were to show.

One of the first acts of the incoming administration was to examine the level of police pay and to improve it at a time of retrenchment in public spending elsewhere and a severe curtailment of salary increases in the public sector. The government made it abundantly clear that it recognized the crucial role of the police in what came to be referred to as the 'fight against crime'. It was also only too aware that, given the experience of the previous decade, a competent, well-paid and well-equipped police force was an absolute necessity if industrial disputes and political demonstrations were not to get out of hand; the Thatcher administration had no intention of enduring the embarrassment of its predecessors, including the Heath government. For while legislation was in train to curb the power of the unions through the processes of the civil law, it would still be necessary to have an alternative device in reserve in the event of what at Saltley had been termed 'mass action'.

The new wave of urban riots

Ironically, the first disorders were not to be industrial but communal. The Brixton riots of 1981, followed by similar disturbances in the Toxteth district of Liverpool were violent and incendiary. Once more the police were under public scrutiny, not least the Metropolitan force whose operation against street crime, code-named 'Swamp 81' was to be identified as the detonator, if not the underlying cause, of the trouble. The scale of the 1981 disturbances was such that Whitelaw's political instinct was to appoint an inquiry which was conducted by Lord Scarman who had the experience of the earlier investigation into the events of Red Lion Square in 1974. In doing so, Whitelaw was following an earlier tradition characteristic of the years of the 'post-war settlement', in distinct contrast to the hawkish approach to public order problems that was consistent with Thatcherite orthodoxy.

The 1981 inquiries into the Brixton and Liverpool disturbances inevitably focused on the behaviour of the police: in London on the attempt to deal with the rising level of street crime by 'saturation' policing and in Liverpool the tactics employed by the police in quelling disorder, including the driving of police vans on to pavements and directly at knots of suspected demonstrators. Neither in Brixton nor in Toxteth were the police popular with the local inhabitants, and in Brixton the racial dimension was central to the conflict. Sir David MacNee, the Metropolitan Commissioner had objected[15] to the use of S.32 of the 1964 Police Act to constitute the inquiry since it gave the appearance that it was police conduct that was at the root of the matter. MacNee was defensive of his force.

Scarman's inquiry was conducted with impeccable objectivity and considerable awareness of the socioeconomic background to the disorders. One of his principal recommendations, that the police should be required to consult periodically with the local community, was subsequently incorporated into the Police and Criminal Evidence Act of 1984.[16] Following Scarman, significant efforts were made in the Metropolitan Police to make consultation effective; unfortunately, they were not to be altogether successful. In 1985, in the course of a raid on a house in Brixton, the mother of the suspect, Mrs Cherry Groce, was accidentally shot and permanently paralysed. The effect of the tragedy was once more to precipitate violence on the streets, again involving serious damage to property, looting, arson and the overturning of cars as well as the hurling of petrol bombs at the police.[17] In the same year, serious disorder occurred in the Handsworth district of Birmingham, again involving arson and looting and resulting in the incineration of two Asian brothers above their shop whom the police were not able to reach and rescue. In London the scene shifted to the Broadwater Farm Estate in Tottenham where, again in the course of a police search, a wholly innocent woman became involved; Mrs Cynthia Jarrett, had a heart attack and died.

The death of Mrs Jarrett acted as a detonator in the volatile atmosphere of this deprived public housing project but, unlike the open streets of Brixton, its architectural design rendered it a readily defensible space for the rioters who were able to hold it against the police who were deployed in large numbers. But if Cynthia Jarrett was to have died of natural causes, albeit in distressing circumstances, Police Constable Blakelock was to die more horribly. For reasons that are still not entirely clear, Blakelock's 'serial'[18] was sent into the estate, detached from the main body of police. It was surrounded and in the course of retreat Blakelock fell, to be engulfed by the crowd. When his body was finally recovered it was clear that, in addition to other serious injuries, an attempt had been made at decapitation.

Not since the death of WPC Yvonne Fletcher, shot from the window of the Libyan People's Bureau in 1984, had the police sustained a casualty so dramatic in its impact. The violence with which Blakelock was killed reflected a degree of pent-up anger in the local community which suggested that police public relations were not all that they might have been. For the residents, some local leaders made remarks that were unhelpful and which they no doubt later regretted.[19] Among the police, on the other hand, there was anger, not only against the inhabitants of Broadwater Farm who for some time after the riot found themselves 'occupied' by large numbers of police, but against senior police officers whom it was alleged had held back a unit of marksmen equipped with baton guns who might have been able to get Blakelock's group out of trouble. To have done so would have meant the use of baton rounds for the first time against a crowd in mainland Britain, a political decision of immense significance.

The problem of firearms and new policing methods

Throughout the 1980s the issues of public order and, in particular, the use of firearms by the police were in the forefront of public consciousness for sustained periods. The tragic accident of the shooting of Mrs Groce was not isolated, for earlier two constables, in a case of mistaken identity, had shot and seriously wounded Stephen Waldorf. They were charged with attempted murder but acquitted. Later, in the West Midlands, while searching for his father who was wanted for a serious crime, a police officer accidentally shot five-year-old John Shorthouse.

The riots of 1981 precipitated a major change in policing methods in the area of public order. As late as 1974 in Red Lion Square, despite the experience of Grosvenor Square in 1968, the police still had no protective headgear and no defensive equipment against missiles or incendiary devices.[20] Nor was there any systematic theory of crowd control that could be translated into action. In 1981 the Association of Chief Police Officers decided to investigate riot control methods that had been developed by the Hong Kong police and these, in due course, were incorporated into what became known as the Tactical Options Manual.[21]

The use of these new techniques first became evident during the miners' strike of 1983–4 at the Orgreave coking plant in Yorkshire. Here, as at Saltley a decade before, there was a major confrontation between police and about 10,000 pickets, but the difference lay in the tactics employed by the police. The television cameras showed police horses cantering into the crowd and, in the words of the Tactical Options Manual, 'creating fear and scattering' it. The use of horses in crowd dispersal is, of course, highly symbolic and redolent of the deployment of the dragoons at Peterloo. Whatever the effect in terms of crowd management, it had the consequence of providing an important entry in the list of incidents to be incorporated into the folk memories of groups on the left of the political spectrum.

While the use of the police in the miners' strike served *inter alia* to deepen the political and social divide in British society in the mid-1980s, it was the deliberate use of riot tactics in an incident in which they were, by any objective test, highly questionable that came to the fore in 1985. This was the occasion of a visit by the Home Secretary, Leon Brittan, to the University of Manchester on 1 March. There had been earlier trouble at Manchester, when during the previous year Michael Heseltine had been showered with red paint, while some weeks before, while at Bradford, John Carlisle, MP, had been attacked while defending economic and social links with South Africa.

A modest group was awaiting Brittan's arrival when about 40 police officers arrived and, without warning, began violently to attack the crowd, throwing people down steps, punching and kicking and using obscene and abusive language. No less disturbing were the allegations that in the following months complainants were assaulted and harrassed, by police officers in plain clothes.

The events in Manchester were to have an even more ironic twist, when one of the principal complainants, Stephen Shaw, found himself in jeopardy of prosecution for attempting to pervert the course of justice. The events in Manchester and the subsequent inquiry which shed little real light on what had gone on, served further to damage the image of policing. It did not, of course, do so in the eyes of those who felt that those who were prepared to use the power of numbers in any extra-parliamentary context, whether as pickets or demonstrators, deserved all that was coming to them.

The Public Order Act 1986

The government response to problems of public order, which had been on its agenda since the early part of the decade, was to legislate in the shape of a new Public Order Act in 1986. So far, the Act has not been employed, as it critics feared, to suppress the legitimate expression of political dissent but it has undoubtedly given the police new powers in the context of controlling demonstrations and, in particular, industrial disputes. In 1986–7 the protracted dispute involving the News International Corporation at Wapping led both to a major strain on police resources in London – as had been the case during the miners' dispute – and to complaints about police behaviour.[22]

Policing demonstrations and industrial disputes is not relished by the majority of senior police officers.[23] For, whatever the causes of public disorders, they are essentially social and political, and ultimately the responsibility of those who, through the exercise of political power in and out of government, shape the nature of society and those events. In this context, the police must be essentially reactive, and to demonstrate the existence of incompetence, corruption or gross impropriety and even violence on the part of policemen does nothing to alter this fact. It is a consequence of the polarization of British society since 1979 that it is increasingly divided into those who believe the police to be nothing but the enthusiastic agents of the Thatcherite New Order and those who perceive them to be the heroic defenders of a civilized society and who, if not entirely blameless, can always be exonerated from any malicious intent.

Perhaps the most striking feature of the police service since 1945 is the growth not merely of professional competence, but of a sense of critical professionalism among its senior ranks. Too many senior officers have been exposed to higher education not to be sceptical or even cynical about the rhetoric of political slogans, and in this respect no force has moved further – or received a greater hammering at the hands of its critics – than the 'Met'. It has not only persevered with attempts to strengthen community relations, often in the face of politically articulated hostility, but it has attempted to take the task of public order policing with great seriousness. At Hounslow, where a replica urban streetscape has been created, complete with shops, houses and flats, there is a programme of continuous training in public order policing which is attended on a continuing basis by officers from each district. In the course of training, in which the officers come under simulated attack with bricks and real petrol bombs, it is possible to develop a high degree of disciplined control, as well as operational efficiency.[24]

The 'Met' enjoys a degree of autonomy not shared by other police forces, which are still accountable in some degree to their police authorities, not all of whom have been enthusiastic in assisting the development of the new style of public order policing.[25] Conflict has been acute in Liverpool and Manchester where an attempt was made to scrap the police band in a cost-cutting exercise after complaints of expenditure on policing the miners' strike. In the West Midlands there was reluctance to purchase riot equipment, and officers drafted into the Handsworth riot had to be equipped with flame-proof overalls borrowed from another force which they literally had to 'try for size' at the scene.[26]

It would be wrong to assume that the admittedly numerous incidents of 'high profile' policing, for all their political significance, constitute the prime concerns of policing in contemporary Britain. The truth is that these are, for the most part, extremely mundane. A diminishing success rate in clearing up reported crime is indicative more of the growth of crime than police inefficiency. In investigations, experiments with tape recording of interviews with suspects and the provision of (the unfortunately termed) 'rape suites' in police stations is evidence of both technical progress and increased social awareness. For, in spite of the extreme political pressures under which the police have been obliged to operate at various times, all the indications are that among those police officers of all ranks who are committed to the traditional concept of policing as a service to the community there is a strong resistance not only to the idea of political interference in operational matters from either the left or the right, but to the imposition of any enveloping ideology.

Police accountability

It is in the Britain of the 1980s as in the third term of Thatcher government its enthusiasts look confidently towards a future in which Thatcherism becomes the sole informing source of social, political and economic ideas, that conflicts about the nature of policing have become acute, simply because the police service represents the primary manifestation of the monopoly of coercive force that is possessed by the state. It is the task of the constable to enforce the law, but in that he is, be he beat officer or Chief Constable, endowed with discretion deriving from an authority which is 'original, not delegated'.[27] He cannot be properly subject to political discretion.

It is in this context that the vexed question of police accountability has to be examined. On the right of the political spectrum it is seen as something owed to government and to the abstraction called the 'state' whose interests are perceived as coterminous with those of the government of the day;[28] on the left, it is seen as a necessary element in a populist conception of how social institutions are legitimated and something which ought to be subject to control by 'ordinary people'. It is in this sense that policing in Britain has never been so close to the heat of the political kitchen since Sir Robert Peel's 'New Police' were castigated in a contemporary broadsheet as 'Raw lobsters, Blue Devils, or by whatever other appropriate Name they may be known'.[29]

Notes

1 See chapter 5.
2 A number of those arrested were held in police custody to be produced at Bow Street court the following morning where the stipendiary magistrate remanded almost all of them in custody. After two days in Brixton prison (it proving extremely difficult for their legal advisers to discover their whereabouts) they reappeared only to be fined. It was an action approved in some quarters for giving them a 'taste of prison'.
3 *Report* (London, HMSO, 1965, Cmnd 2735). For another complexion on the affair see Mary Grigg, *The Challenor Case*, (London, Penguin, 1965).
4 By no means entirely by students. At the LSE, for example, those who wielded the pick-axes and crowbars to break down the notorious 'gates' included an assortment of roughnecks, some of them IRA 'collectors' from the Barbican building site.
5 There rapidly grew up a mythology about the Grosvenor Square demonstrations but the romanticized versions only recount tales

of police brutality of which there were some undoubted instances. But the fury of some demonstrators not only in their attacks on the police, but on vehicles parked in adjoining streets, was equally noteworthy. Some of the demonstrators seemed to identify the Metropolitan Police as the surrogates of the US administration.

6 At Red Lion Square the right-wing supporters of the National Front were as enthusiastic for violence as their opponents.

7 *Report* (London, HMSO, 1975, Cmnd 5919).

8 An account of the events of 1974 is contained in Stuart Hall, *Policing the Crisis* (London, Macmillan, 1978).

9 Neither of these views does justice to the position of the police. To have stood back from the 'mass action' of the pickets at Saltley or Grunwick would have been to permit one interest group to impose its will upon another by force of numbers. The attempts to keep the Saltley plant open and to get the workers into the Grunwick factory, though unpalatable to the strikers, were nevertheless lawful and the use of force to frustrate those intentions by force or the threat of it, unequivocally unlawful. The situation would be the same if the National Front attempted to besiege the offices of the NCCL or an anti-apartheid group. What happened at Wapping in 1986–7 was that the police would not permit the pickets to approach and speak to the drivers of the TNT trucks carrying the newspapers to attempt to persuade them to desist. On the contrary, the trucks were allowed to approach and leave the News International plant at high speed.

10 The Chief Constable of Greater Manchester, Mr James Anderton, who has spoken of his sense of divine inspiration as well as having pronounced on the problem of AIDS.

11 The Special Patrol Group (SPG) was formed in April 1965 as a tactical reserve to be deployed throughout the 'Met'. Highly mobile in Ford Transit vans, they became unpopular with the public in deprived areas when used, for example, in drugs raids. Ordinary beat officers were often unenthusiastic about them and referred to them as 'The Cowboys'.

12 National Council for Civil Liberties, *Southall 23 April 1979* (London, NCCL, 1980).

13 See Gilbert Kelland, *Crime in London* (London, Bodley Head, 1986). Also Maurice Punch, *Conduct Unbecoming* (London and New York, Tavistock, 1985), and Dick Hobbs, *Doing the Business* (Oxford, Clarendon Press, 1988).

14 Ibid., p. 230.

15 See chapter 5, note 25.

16 *The Brixton Disorders 10–12 April 1981* (London, HMSO, 1982, Cmnd 8427).

17 In one incident a huge cylindrical rubbish skip on castors was filled with blazing material including petrol and run into the police lines.
18 The term used to describe the smallest unit of deployment.
19 Allegations were also made that suspects arrested in the course of the investigation into Blakelock's murder were held illegally in detention without access to lawyers. The propriety of the conviction of those charged in connection with his death has also been challenged in some quarters.
20 At a disturbance at the Notting Hill Carnival in 1976 the police were obliged to pick up dustbin lids in an attempt to protect themselves from the hail of missiles.
21 This proved to be a source of friction between government and opposition when the Shadow Home Secretary was denied a sight of it, although sections were produced in evidence during the trials of miners arrested at Orgreave in 1984. For an account of the development of this style of public order policing, see Gerry Northam, 'A fair degree of force', *The Listener*, 31 October 1985, and his book *Shooting in the Dark: Riot Police in Britain* (London, Faber and Faber, 1988).
22 The major disturbance at Wapping was on the night of 24 January, 1987 – the first anniversary of the move of News International papers to the Wapping site and the sackings of some 5000 staff. About 12,000 demonstrators were present; 162 police officers were injured and 67 people arrested of whom 65 were subsequently convicted. There were also allegations of serious misconduct on the part of the police and after protracted investigations of these complaints by officers from Northamptonshire on behalf of the Police Complaints Authority 18 constables, four sergeants, one woman constable and one inspector were charged in January 1989 with a variety of offences including assault, perjury and conspiracy to pervert the course of justice.
23 A senior Metropolitan officer confided to me during the miners' strike that he was 'fed up with being a member of Maggie Thatcher's private army'.
24 The breakdown of control at the basic level is almost certainly the primary source of gratuitous violence. Initially, a large number of injuries were sustained during training. This has been dramatically reduced at Hounslow; in contrast, the Manchester force has eschewed such realism and officers in training hurl bags of flour at each other.
25 For an excellent account of these matters see Ian Oliver, *Police, Government and Accountability* (London, Macmillan, 1987).

26 Personal conversation with the Chief Constable of the West Midlands Police.

27 See chapter 5 note 32.

28 As defined by the judge at the trial of Clive Ponting in 1984.

29 Broadsheet dated 10 November 1830, 'Eliz. Soulby, Printer, 91, Gracechurch Street', reproduced in David Ascoli, *The Queen's Peace* (London, Hamish Hamilton, 1979) between pp. 146 and 147.

11 From Consensus to Division

It is now a political commonplace that the basis of what has come to be known as the 'post-war settlement' has been eroded to the point where it no longer exists. Whereas in the Britain of 1945 there were genuine political divisions, there was also a broad measure of agreement between government and opposition with regard to both the ground rules of political initiative and the general shape of the society that was desired. Where there was disagreement in the field of criminal justice it was about methods rather than objectives and about the pace rather than the nature of change. Issues such as capital punishment which were highly controversial came to be seen primarily as issues of conscience and not of party loyalty.

The conformation of political life in Britain has changed, almost out of recognition in that neither the Labour nor the Conservative parties of the late 1980s bear more than a superficial resemblance to their counterparts in 1945 or even in 1965. The nature of economic and social change has been no less profound: from an immediate post-war period in which assumptions about full employment were common to all parties, Britain has moved to a position in which its North Sea oil revenues have become more important than its heavy manufacturing output as a source of earnings as the once dominant industries of shipbuilding, mining and motor manufacture have declined; and to a position in which the market in financial services has become a dominant feature of the economy. For the first time since the industrial revolution, Britain has become a net importer of manufactured goods. The consequences of these economic changes have been profound, bringing poverty and unemployment to what were once the centres of wealth creation and increasing affluence to the 'Golden Triangle' of south-east England. It can be argued that the way we live today is so different from life in the heyday of the post-war settlement that the emergence of new institutional arrangements is entirely rational and desirable.

If the consensus which once existed is no longer relevant to issues relating to criminal justice the question must be posed whether the change has come about as a result of something intrinsic in the nature of the problems of criminal justice or whether they arise from another source. In attempting to answer this question, it is necessary to look at the events of the past nine years, not as if Margaret Thatcher had arrived on the scene as some *deus ex machina* in 1979, but as the consequences of what had gone before.

In this book the year 1960 has frequently been used as a point at which to demonstrate the differences between the world of Britain immediately after the war and that of the country which had not only put austerity aside but which was moving – initially at any rate – into a period of exponential economic growth. The late 1940s and 1950s were years dominated by recollections of the war and the heyday of politicians and administrators whose ideas had been shaped in a much earlier period. The judges especially, as we have seen, were a group dominated by old men with very traditional ideas. The period of the 1960s, in contrast, was buoyed up not only by an unprecedented experience of economic growth and newly acquired wealth, but by a new spirit of progressive liberalism that was particularly manifested in reforms of the criminal law that affected private morality, such as obscenity, homosexuality, abortion and gambling.

But a novel combination of long-term economic phenomena, such as the terminal decline of Britain's traditional manufacturing base, and the short-term effects of the oil crisis of the 1970s clouded the once bright prospect. In contrast to the 1960s, the ensuing decade became increasingly gloomy. Inflation, industrial unrest, the apparent inability of governments to govern, whether headed by Heath or Callaghan, all contributed to a sense of malaise. It was a mood shared in the United

States where the combination of political humiliation after defeat in Vietnam and economic recession made 'walking tall' increasingly uncommon. The appeal of Reaganism, like that of Thatcherism, based upon a restatement of *laisser-faire* economics combined with sufficient government intervention to propel all things marketwards was irresistibly – some would say fatally – attractive. In 1979, the electorate that only a few months before had been impotently enduring a 'winter of discontent' had the opportunity of endorsing a new approach. The package included the prospect of controlling not only the overweening power of trade unions that could make the lives of ordinary citizens miserable by depriving them of electricity and commuter trains but that of the street criminals and the burglars. Not a few electors hoped that the new government would restore capital punishment, at the very least for Irish terrorists and other violent political activists. In the course of this political sea change the period of the 1960s was increasingly identified as one of moral decline and the root of many of Britain's troubles.

In the field of criminal justice penal reformers were castigated as 'do-gooders'. Punishment, rather than 'treatment', became the preferred objective for the penal system. Meanwhile, those responsible for the institutions of criminal justice, especially those in the prison service, recognized that they had been overwhelmed by the sheer pressure of numbers to the point where the ideal of rehabilitation was becoming an increasingly unattainable aspiration. The prison crisis grew in such a way as to produce changes that are now almost certainly irreversible.

The growth of crime and the decline of the 'rehabilitative ideal' have gone hand in hand for almost a decade, but it would be wrong to assume that the first was the cause of the second. In the decade after 1945 the growth of crime did not significantly deter optimism among the Prison Commissioners or most of the staff working in the probation or prison services from believing that the reform of offenders was both a legitimate and attainable goal. The climate of the 1960s, notwithstanding the continued growth of crime, was so predominantly liberal and progressive that to have abandoned the idea would have been unthinkable.

The 1960s have been castigated as the years of permissive-ness', almost as if there had been a conspiracy actively to undermine the traditional values of public morality and family life, to promote sexual licence and deviance as intrinsically desirable. But it is also possible to see the decade as a period in which the virtues of tolerance were promoted. For not only was Britain becoming an increasingly diversified society in terms of its ethnic composition and more cosmopolitan as more people gained experience of a world beyond Britain's shores as a result of the foreign travel that they could newly afford. Such experiences stimulated the notion that there might be other forms of diversity that deserved recognition.

The reform of the laws relating to homosexuality, abortion and censorship in the theatre should therefore be seen in the context of new definitions of tolerance and freedom. And here there is a paradox for the philosophy of the New Right that sees the marketplace as the ultimate source of all social and political legitimacy. For, if men are to be free to conduct economic relations, untrammelled by any interference from the state, by what reasoning are they not permitted the same freedom to govern their private behaviour? If competition is to be encouraged, why should it not include the competitive sale of drugs which individuals should be free to consume or not, as they choose?

During the period discussed in this book there was a change from 'traditional' values (in reality those of a dominant upper middle class which had been ascendant since the Victorian middle classes emerged as the most forceful and articulate section of society) to those which were more tolerant, if not necessarily approving, of cultural and moral diversity. But since the late 1970s there has been a return to a combination of economic individualism and a more restrictive personal morality.

All such discussions, if they are linked to the theme of crime and its control, assume that the majority of those committing offences are carried along in the main currents of social change. But the contrary may be true. The sub-culture of crime has an astonishing persistence. There is little, save the nature of the goods, that separates Jonathan Wilde in eighteenth-century London from his modern counterpart who buys in stolen goods at a discount and sells them on at a profit. There is little difference between the street criminal of early Victorian London who came upon his victim by surprise and the contemporary thief who snatches a handbag on the escalator of the Underground. Nothing about the rapist has changed and remarkably little about the burglar. Criminal activity is, in this sense, both permanent and parasitic and, since so much of it is economically significant, its incidence is inevitably related to the available volume of property at risk. Property crime has, too, to be seen as a form of redistribution, albeit on the dark side of the law.

The control of crime, in contrast to crime itself, is subject to more variable fashions. Since 1945 the notion that it is primarily the business of the police has been an accepted belief which few have ever thought to challenge. Yet the progressive decline in the clear-up rate, notwithstanding increases in police manpower and resources, suggests that the belief is ill founded. Physical methods of crime control are more effective than policemen, certainly where property is concerned, and even such mundane things as the improvement of street lighting and the intelligent design of public space can reduce crimes of assault. Policing has emerged as being, in the long run, more relevant to the maintenance of public order.

Compared with their counterparts of 1945, the police are incomparably more powerful in terms of their coercive potential, not merely in terms of legislated authority, but in operational sophistication. Seen in one perspective, the Chief Constables of Britain have more effective forces at their disposal, to be deployed with a greater degree of independence and autonomy, than the landed barons of the early Middle Ages. For the vexed question of the accountability of the police service remains a permanent item on the political agenda, at the heart of the conflict between central and local government and presenting the theory of populist democracy with one of its most serious challenges. In the 1960s the debate had been about police corruption, but that referred to the failings of individual officers. The contemporary debate about accountability relates not to corruption, but to the definition of the limits of police power. How far can the police retain a credible degree of political independence when they become involved in social conflicts which are themselves so highly charged with a political potential? It is a question which is not settled by much of the contemporary political rhetoric. For when those on the left argue that the police are but the servants of bourgeois capitalism they frequently do so in the confident belief that in their view certain disorders are legitimate; 'mass action', for example, is seen as having an ethical legitimacy if it serves the interests of the working class. The right, in contrast, sees the interests of the propertied classes as coterminous with the interests of the state, and *vice versa*. For those on the right, allegations of police impropriety are an attack upon the police as the custodians of order. Blair Peach had actually travelled to Southall and Kevin Gately had chosen to go to Red Lion Square; no one made them go. Similarly, if the students who were assaulted by the Manchester police in 1985 had been studying instead of waiting for Leon Brittan, they would have not gone home beaten and bruised.

The same kinds of political division may be discerned with regard to the prison crisis. The left makes considerable play of the fact that a greater than expected proportion of ethnic minorities is denied bail or is sent to prison and sees this in terms of the oppression of the political system. Similarly, feminist groups are concerned about the presence of women in institutions. Those at the other end of the spectrum take the simple view that those who are in prison deserve to be there, and that they have a choice of whether to commit crime or not. There are flaws in both sets of arguments. The courts seldom rise to the degree of conscious sophistication necessary to decide that this or that offender is a proper case for 'oppression'. Most of the time those who send people to prison do so because they cannot think of anything else to do with them.

It is in the context of the decline of the prison system that the demise of liberal humanitarianism, which dominated the 1950s and 1960s, is most clearly seen. The level of squalor to which the local prison has sunk would have been past the belief of those running them 40 years ago, yet the increasingly shocking reports of the Inspector of Prisons produce scarcely a ripple in public consciousness. This is not an indifference that is confined to prisons. As the great Victorian mental hospitals are closed and their homeless and socially isolated patients decanted into the community, increasing numbers of them appear to find shelter under arches and sleep in cardboard boxes. Waterloo and the South Bank are littered with this pathetic human detritus. Yet their plight is not on any central political agenda. Nor is their presence seen any longer as a problem for the police who, even 20 years ago, would have been 'moving them on'. There is a distinction drawn between the deserving and the undeserving which grows more narrow and less realistic. Prisoners are 'undeserving', even if a proportion of them are the vagrant ex-mental patients who are still mentally ill. The homeless and the unemployed are conditionally deserving if they can demonstrate efforts on their part to improve their lot. Those who sink back into the torpor of hopelessness are likely to find themselves re-categorized. The belief that 'there is work for anyone who wants it' is constantly reinforced by reference to the advertisements for work that fill the columns of newspapers and cover the walls of job centres.

Perhaps the most important change that has occurred since the mid-1970s has been the steady growth of a new underclass in British society, often homeless, almost always jobless and with an increasing dependence on public welfare. It naturally gravitates to urban centres where all marginal groups have the best chance of survival. It includes many who are young and demographically it is reproductive. Its dependence upon welfare is likely to diminish not on account of a new-found self-sufficiency, but because of a reduction in the quantum of welfare itself, part of the contemporary pattern of wealth redistribution from the poor to the rich. As such, the new underclass must turn as it has always done throughout history to a combination of crime and street trade, the two interconnected and sometimes indistinguishable, part of the trade including a growth of prostitution. In its predatory nature it follows a natural instinct for survival, just as the fox, driven from its natural habitat by modern farming methods, becomes a suburban creature living from scraps and dustbins.

The new underclass is likely to become the predominant group in the declining areas of the inner city from which the middle and employed working classes have increasingly removed themselves, leaving only the super-rich secure in their defensible space. The pattern of great American cities like New York seems set to be followed in London. But, perhaps more important, the new underclass is likely to constitute a permanently unstable and at times unpredictably volatile element in political life. There is no reason to be optimistic in thinking that the events of Brixton, Handsworth or Broadwater Farm will never recur.

It is in this context that the shape of policing and social control in general is likely to be determined. There is, of course, a distinction to be made between crime control and the maintenance of public order; the former may become a diminishing interest of the police and the latter a growing concern. Similarly with imprisonment. At some stage it is likely that diversion from imprisonment will become a practical and economic neccessity, irrespective of its ethical desirability, and imprisonment will become increasingly reserved for those who are deemed to be a danger rather than a nuisance.

As the decade of the 1980s approaches its end, the problems of the prison system in Britain remain apparently as intractable as ever. However much the courts have attempted to respond to the exhortations of ministers and reformers alike to be sparing in the use of custody, both for remand prisoners and for those convicted, the size of the incarcerated population has continued to grow. Prison staff have been reluctant to cooperate in confining ever more inmates into already overcrowded local and remand prisons. One result has been to make the detention of prisoners in police cells a normal feature of the system.

Politically, there is little mileage for any government in being seen to be concerned about the humanitarian aspects of prison conditions; for the Thatcher administration there is, however, another dimension: its commitment to maintaining a high profile for 'law and order' issues as part of an overall electoral strategy. In an address to the Conservative Party Conference at Brighton in October 1988, for which she received a standing ovation lasting almost nine minutes, Margaret Thatcher maintained that Conservatism had a traditional claim to the 'middle ground' in British society. Part of that 'middle ground' is, of course, a concern about crime (and often homespun solutions to the problem) and also that what is done by the state should represent some concessions to practical rationality where policy and expenditure are concerned. The problem for the Thatcher government is not just that prison conditions are disgracefully insanitary and wretched but that they represent a considerable outlay of public resources with astonishingly little to show by way of practical results.

Leon Brittan had enjoyed a bubble popularity with the

Conference in 1983; Douglas Hurd's ovation at Brighton in 1988 represented more than just approval for his speech. Indeed, given that Hurd, speaking as Home Secretary, had recently made one of the most articulate statements of opposition to capital punishment, his ability to hold his ground with authority with an audience that was the next day to jeer and catcall Edward Heath was all the more remarkable. Like almost every Conservative Home Secretary of stature since the war, he has been suspected, if not of 'closet liberalism', then at least of being the prisoner of his 'liberal' Civil Service advisers. From what he had to say, it became clear that the government intended to tackle with some resolution the problem of prison overcrowding and to develop new means of dealing with offenders in the community.

The passage in Hurd's speech which attracted the headlines was his proposal experimentally to introduce the electronic 'tagging' of remand prisoners as an alternative to holding them in prison. Tagging has been developed in the United States and employed with varying degrees of success. It might properly be described as a 'hi-tech' electronic version of the traditional ball and chain though physically less irksome. Strong objections to the idea have been voiced by civil libertarians and by members of the probation service. It remains to be seen whether technically it can be feasibly introduced into Britain and it is these issues, rather than those of civil liberty, that are likely to affect the ultimate decision on the future of the scheme. But it was in July 1988 that the government published its two radical sets of proposals that are likely to have more far-reaching consequences than electronic tagging.

Two Green Papers, *Private Sector Involvement in the Remand System*[1] and *Punishment, Custody and the Community*,[2] set out a series of highly radical proposals which, if implemented, are likely to set a stamp upon the character of the criminal justice system no less unambiguously Thatcherite than that which privatization has put upon the monopolistic provision of public utilities such as gas, telephones, electricity and water. That by the time of the publication of the Green Paper on remand privatization there were already in place two companies (one with American links) ready and willing to undertake the task is indicative of the extent to which the publication of this consultative document had been regarded as the symbolic preliminary to legislation that would follow as surely as night follows day. The Green Paper makes the assumption that operating under the constraints of the market, the private contractor is able to be more cost effective: 'Recruitment and deployment of staff may be more flexible'.[3] While the idea that only servants of the state should be responsible for prisoners is not dismissed out of hand, the paper makes it clear that the government does not regard it as any constitutional impediment. Rather, the privatization of remand prisons has to be seen in the more general context of Thatcherite ideology in which the activities of the state should be limited to controlling the central agencies of legitimate coercion – the armed forces and the police – and to generally directing the shape of social institutions through legislation that permits an ever-increasing scope for government by 'agency'. Since such agencies will be, by definition, drawn from the private sector, they are warranted in their efficiency by the axiomatic impeccability of all that is and has its being in the marketplace.

In more practical terms, and at least one back-bench MP has suggested as much, privatization will severely limit the power of the Prison Officers' Association. The POA has been a thorn in the flesh of both Home Office ministers and civil servants for the past decade. As far as government is concerned, it represents the kind of Civil Service union that exemplifies the abuse of union power, that is, being possessed of a capacity to frustrate the wishes of its employer. Under privatization, the power of the union will be broken if only because the new contractors will be able to take advantage of the government's own trade union legislation to ensure that the POA goes unrecognized and where possible will recruit either non-union labour or include no-strike clauses in contractual arrangements. What is likely is that once the remand system has been privatized, the new penal corporations will seek to expand into the building and running of prisons for convicted prisoners, as they have in the United States, and also to diversify by providing non-custodial services as well.

This possibility is clearly indicated in the Green Paper

Punishment, Custody and the Community. For some time it has been in the mind of ministers to toughen up non-custodial sentences, such as community service, while at the same time encouraging the courts to make greater use of non-custodial sentences to ease the pressure on prisons. In a keynote speech to the Association of Chief Probation Officers in Leeds in September 1988, John Patten, the Minister of State, made it clear that the probation service would need to become involved in overtly punitive forms of non-custodial sentence. He urged the Chief Probation Officers to explain the new ideas in the Green Paper to their subordinates and to translate them into practice. The National Association of Probation Officers took a different view, rejecting the notion that punishment should make an offender's life 'gratutiously difficult and unpleasant'.[4] At its Conference in October 1988 the Association made clear its grave reservations about electronic tagging and some probation officers have already indicated their intention not to cooperate with the scheme.

The Green Papers of July 1988, both indicative of the shape of legislation to come, must also represent important sentences written upon the wall for both the Prison and Probation Officers' Associations. Just as privatized prisons sound the death knell of POA power, so *Punishment, Custody and the Community* in a single paragraph indicates a similar fate for a recalcitrant probation service.[5] It refers to a new body to organize punishment in the community which would not itself supervise offenders directly, but which would contract for services. In the process of tendering the probation service would have to compete with other agencies, including those from the private sector.

In this brief paragraph a prospect for the criminal justice system in the twenty-first century assumes a third-dimensional reality which goes to the very heart of the question of the state's constitutional monopoly of the formal coercion of its citizens. To what extent is it entitled to delegate its authority and under what conditions and with what safeguards of freedom under the law? The historical experience of commercial penology is replete with instances of incompetence, cruelty, corruption and inefficiency. That the state assumed its penal monopoly in the eighteenth and nineteenth centuries was indicative of the fact that the servants of the state could not only perform the various tasks more effectively but could be more readily monitored for incompetence and impropriety. The commercial prison operator of the late twentieth century has, as yet, no track record to be compared with the earlier sorry tale, although remand facilities could provide useful opportunities for the imposition of charges for special services for food and recreation, just as fees for the casting off of irons and the provision of candles proved an important source of income for the gaolers of Newgate and the Fleet. There may be good commercial reasons for privatizing large sectors of the criminal justice system, including the courts, but the ultimate justification must include some reference to considerations of political philosophy. The problem with philosophy, of course, is that it tends to raise questions rather than answer them, something unlikely to endear the exercise to those who favour ideological solutions to social questions that have the comforting certitude of a nautical almanac.

Nor are innovations likely to be confined to prisons and the treatment of offenders in the community. Although the Thatcher administration originally gave the impression that as far as police budgets were concerned the 'sky was the limit', since 1983 it has given much closer scrutiny to how the money is being spent. The police portion of the 'law and order' budget increased from £1.4bn in 1970–1 to £3.5bn in 1987–8. The Home Office Circular No.114 of 1983 made it clear to Chief Constables that unless the Home Secretary was satisfied that existing resources were being used to advantage, no authorization would be given for an increase in police manpower. The Audit Commission in 1988 undertook a wide ranging study of police financial management and the role of Her Majesty's Inspectorate of Constabulary is under review. It is not only clear that the government is interested in financial compctence; it has an interest in the culture of police working practices, some of them hallowed by generations of policemen and coming close to some of the 'Spanish customs' that have characterized other highly integrated and unionized workplaces. At the 1988 conference of the Police Federation, Hurd made it clear that time honoured allowances, including those for notional housing costs, would not be excluded from scrutiny. At the same time, police effectiveness in controlling crime appears to be in decline as is reflected in statements like that of the Chief Constable of Sussex, that 'the police are losing control of the streets'; there is pressure towards the increasing use of private security services to protect shopping precincts, residential property and even areas of public space. That is a development feared by the Police Federation no less than the privatization of prisons raises the anxiety of the prison officers.

The legal profession has always operated in a marketplace, albeit with a mass of restrictive practices. In October 1988 the Lord Chancellor, Lord Mackay of Clashfern, announced that the government was planning the most fundamental reform of the profession in this century. A Green Paper was planned for January 1989 and after a period of three months for consultation the government proposed to legislate in the 1989–90 parliamentary session. The anticipated changes will not only alter the structure of the profession, especially the inter-relationship between solicitors and barristers, but will almost certainly sharpen the commercial profile of legal services. In this, of course, there are parallels with the medical profession, many of whose members enjoy the benefits that derive from the expanding marketplace of commercial health care. The future for legal aid is therefore somewhat uncertain. Not all Law Centres have been popular among government supporters, especially those subsidized by left-wing local authorities that specialize in work involving the rights of tenants and welfare claimants. How far the right to legal representation, like the right to health care is actually a 'right' or merely a good that must be bought in the market like any other commodity or service is increasingly unclear. If legal aid arrangements are to exist in the future it seems likely that they will be categorized as a form of welfare benefit for those of limited means whose provision is justified less in terms of benevolence than that of the general efficiency of the legal system: it is as logical for the state to provide its penniless citizens with the marketable expertise of lawyers as it is to provide them with commercial prisons.

There remains the question of capital punishment. It is an issue which is omnipresent even though the death penalty was abolished 20 years ago and the last executions carried out in 1964. The public has never ceased to prefer it for the crimes it considers most heinous and the issue has been before the

House of Commons no fewer than 19 times since 1957, six of them since July 1979, the last being by way of an amendment to the Criminal Justice Bill on 7 June 1988. Since 1979, the majorities against the death penalty have been substantial: 119 in 1979; 162 in 1982; 145 in 1983; 112 in 1987. In 1988, the majority was 123.[6] The lowest majority, on 3 April 1987 of 112, was still greater than the Conservative majority in the House.

The position of capital punishment in the politics of criminal justice is one of paradox. Now it is essentially a problem for the Conservative party alone for the death penalty has no support on the opposition benches.[7] In spite of what is perceived to be an increasingly right-wing intake on to the Conservative back-benches since 1979 and the Prime Minister's unswerving personal support for capital punishment, the government has eschewed a populist reflex to incorporate restoration in the context of a government Bill. For not only is there substantial support for the status quo among many senior back-benchers of the Heath era, including former ministers, but the Cabinet is itself divided. Most significant in the 1988 debate was the intervention of the Home Secretary, Douglas Hurd, in taking a view diametrically opposed to Margaret Thatcher's. And while advocates of the death penalty were reported to have said that after their last defeat they 'would be back', the principle of the issue being the subject of a free vote seems now to be so well established that it would be impossible for this or any future government to insist otherwise. Thus, in a sense, capital punishment remains perhaps the last issue to be debated in the spirit of the 'post-war settlement' and the divided conscience of the parliamentary Conservative party its still vibrant symbol.

Notes

1 London, HMSO, 1988, Cmnd 434.
2 London, HMSO, 1988, Cmnd 424.
3 *Private Sector Involvement in the Remand System* (London, HMSO, 1988, Cmnd 434), paras 44–52.
4 *NAPO News*, no. 4, October 1988 (The Bulletin of the National Association of Probation Officers).

5 *Punishment, Custody and the Community* (London, HMSO, 1988, Cmnd 424), para. IV 44.

6 On one of these six occasions, 10 April 1986, a new clause in the Armed Forces Bill expressly to abolish capital punishment for certain military offences was heavily defeated. Strictly speaking, of course, the abolition of capital punishment has always meant capital punishment for murder but there have been no executions for crimes against military discipline since the war just as the last executions for treason – of Joyce and Amery – were in 1945. In interpreting the votes, however, it must be borne in mind that they have not all been on the single and simple issue of whether the death penalty should be reintroduced or not; only that of 9 July 1979 was a 'vote in principle'. In May 1982 and July 1983 there were numerous amendments relating to categories of capital murder, and in June 1988 the purpose of the amendment was to empower juries to recommend the death sentence – a proposal to which the Lord Chief Justice, Lord Lane, was reported to be wholly opposed. What is also perhaps significant about the 1988 debate was the suggestion, floated in various quarters, that death need not be by hanging, but by more 'humane' methods such as lethal injection. Experience of this method of execution in the United States, where it has been introduced, suggests that far from being 'more humane' it is proving to be more barbaric in its detailed administration than either electrocution or the gas chamber. The Gowers Commission maintained, probably rightly, that of all methods of execution hanging was the speediest and least distressing for the condemned.

7 In 1979 and 1982 a solitary Labour member voted for capital punishment, and until 1987 one Liberal member voted in similar fashion.

Appendix

Prime Ministers; Home Secretaries and Lords Chief Justice; 1945–1988

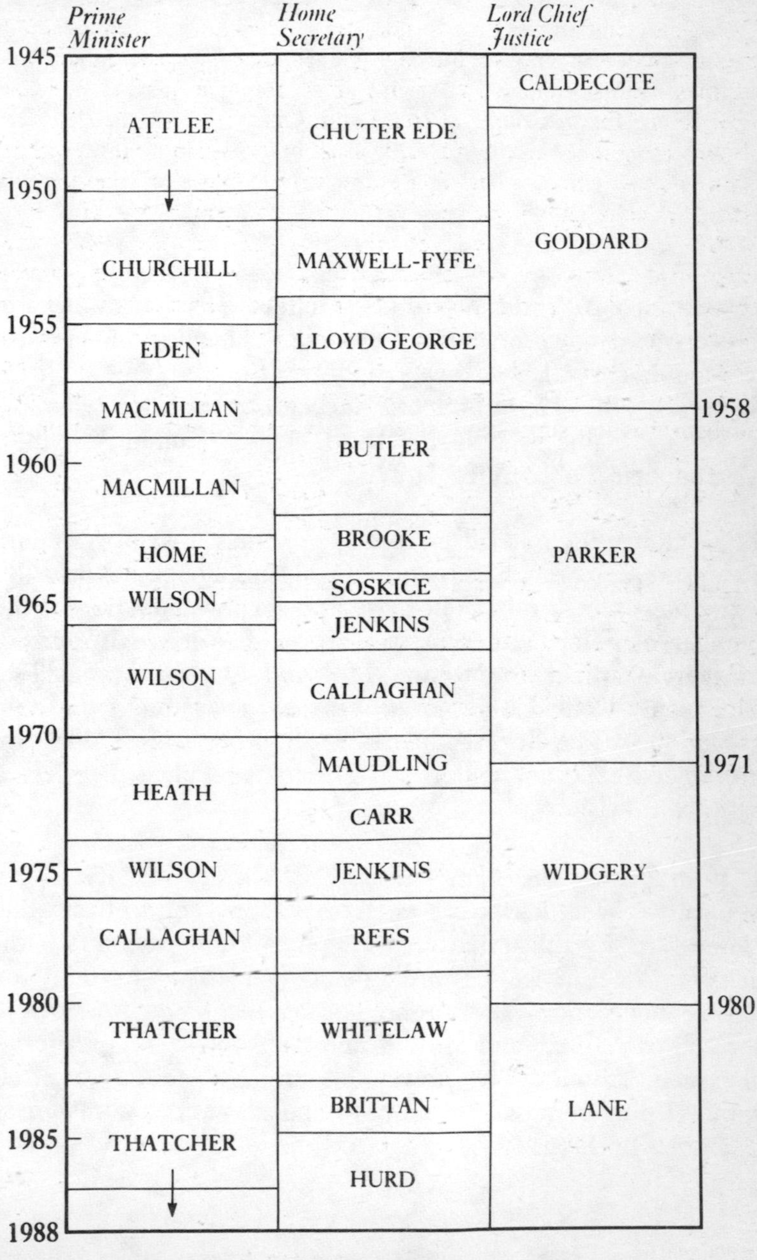
Prime Minister
Home Secretary
Lord Chief Justice
1945
ATTLEE
CHUTER EDE
CALDECOTE
1950
CHURCHILL
MAXWELL-FYFE
GODDARD
1955
EDEN
LLOYD GEORGE
MACMILLAN
1958
1960
MACMILLAN
BUTLER
HOME
BROOKE
PARKER
1965
WILSON
SOSKICE
JENKINS
WILSON
CALLAGHAN
1970
HEATH
MAUDLING
1971
CARR
1975
WILSON
JENKINS
WIDGERY
CALLAGHAN
REES
1980
THATCHER
WHITELAW
1980
BRITTAN
LANE
1985
THATCHER
HURD
1988

Outline Chronology

1945 Second World War ends. General election in Britain: first Labour government to command majority in House of Commons with 146 seats. Chuter Ede appointed Home Secretary. Sir Harold Scott succeeds Air Vice Marshal Sir Philip Game as only the third civilian Commissioner of Metropolitan Police since 1829.

1946 Rayner Goddard succeeds Thomas Inskip, Viscount Caldecote, as Lord Chief Justice of England. Police Act provides for modest increase in police pay and for the reduction of the number of police forces in England and Wales. Murders of Margery Gardner in Notting Hill and Doreen Marshall in Branksome Dene Chine, Bournemouth; subsequent trial and execution of Neville Heath. Six Labrador retriever dogs are introduced experimentally by Metropolitan Police to selected suburban divisions.

1948 Opening of National Police College at Ryton on Dunsmore, Warwickshire; to be removed in 1960 to Bramshill, Hampshire. Establishment of the Oaksey committee on conditions of police service. Criminal Justice Act passed: introduction of detention centres and attendance centres, a new sentence of corrective training and modification of system of preventive detention. Abolition of powers of criminal courts to order corporal punishment. Attempts to abolish capital punishment frustrated by House of Lords.

1949 Appointment of Royal Commission on Capital Punishment (Chairman, Sir Ernest Gowers; Secretary, Francis Graham-Harrison). Legal Aid and Advice Act. Timothy Evans convicted in November of the murder of his baby daughter Geraldine at 10 Rillington Place, Notting Hill.

1950 Timothy Evans hanged for murder in March at Pentonville Prison.

1951 Recorded indictable crime figures reach all-time high of 524,506 for England and Wales. Subsequent fall-off until 1955 when figures begin to climb again.

1952 Great London 'smog' in November lasting nine days and causing major traffic problems. Police effectiveness severely restricted. Rapid rise in breakings into premises and crimes of assault producing abnormal crime figures for the month. Death of PC Miles in December attending scene of break-in at Barlow and Parker's warehouse, Tamworth Road, Croydon. Arrest of Christopher Craig and Derek Bentley.

1953 Christopher Craig (aged 16) convicted of murder of PC Miles and sentenced to be detained at Her Majesty's Pleasure. Derek Bentley (aged 19) sentenced to death and executed. Public outcry at Bentley's execution: crowds demonstrate outside Wandsworth Prison and smash noticeboard displaying statement that sentence has been carried out. Motion in July for leave to bring in Bill to suspend death penalty for five years defeated in House of Commons by 256 to 195 votes. Conviction in June of John Reginald Halliday Christie following his plea of guilty but insane to the murder of no fewer than six women whose remains were found buried beneath the floor and in the garden of 10 Rillington Place, Notting Hill. Maxwell-Fyfe, Home Secretary, appoints David Scott-Henderson, QC, to inquire into the cases of Christie and Evans in private and to determine whether there might have been a miscarriage of justice (6–13 July). 14 July, Scott-Henderson exonerates official conduct of the Evans case. 15 July, Christie hanged at Pentonville. Publication of Report of Royal Commission on Capital Punishment in September. Suggests that no significant reform of the law of murder is practically possible, short of abolition, rejecting as impractical the recognition of 'degrees' of murder. House of Lords debates Report of Royal Commission in December.

1954 Prosecution of Martin Secker and Warburg Ltd for publication of *The Philanderer*. Notable interpretation of the law of obscenity by Mr Justice Stable.

1955 House of Commons debates Report of Royal Commission on Capital Punishment in February. Lloyd George, Home Secretary, moves that the House does no more than 'take note' of its recommendations. Sydney Silverman proposes abolitionist amendment to government motion: defeated by 245 to 214 votes. In April Ruth Ellis shoots dead her lover, David Blakeney outside a pub in Hampstead. Ruth Ellis convicted and sentenced to death in June. Petition of some 2,000 signatures presented for her reprieve. On 13 July Ruth Ellis hanged at Holloway Prison. Crowd of 500 keeps overnight vigil at prison gates swelled by a further 1,000 as hour of execution approaches, chanting 'Evans! Bentley! Ellis!' Massive press coverage and comment in Britain and abroad. In November abolitionists lose attempt to introduce private member's bill for abolition. Government rejects all proposals of Royal Commission. Silverman Abolition Bill gets first reading under 10 Minute Rule: defeated at second reading. In December Oxford Union Debate on capital punishment: motion 'to abolish the death penalty forthwith' passed by 378 to 161 votes.

1956 In January, Inns of Court Conservative Society publishes pamphlet on law of murder suggesting modifications to the law. Government motion in February to amend the law on murder along lines suggested by the Society defeated by 293 to 262 votes. Government promises facilities and free vote for Silverman abolition bill. In June Silverman Bill passes Commons third reading by 152 votes to 133. In July, House of Lords rejects Silverman Bill by 238 to 95 votes. Conservative Party Conference of October opposes abolition but agrees to limitation of death penalty. Government's own Homicide Bill given unopposed second reading in Commons in November. Disciplinary proceedings against Chief Constable of Cardiganshire alleging incompetence. Amalgamation of force with neighbouring Carmarthenshire.

1957 In March Homicide Act becomes law establishing categories of capital and non-capital murder and new defences of provocation and diminished responsibility. Prosecution of Chief Constable of Brighton and two detectives for corruption: detectives convicted and imprisoned but Chief Constable acquitted. Court criticizes Chief Constable who is dismissed by Watch Committee. Chief Constable sues. House of Lords rules that his dismissal was a breach of rules of natural justice. Prosecution and imprisonment for fraud of Chief Constable of Worcester. Allegations by John Waters of Thurso against police. Home Secretary, R. A. Butler, sets up inquiry under Tribunals of Evidence Act 1921. Allegations against PC Eastmond of the Metropolitan Police involving alleged assaults by and against one Garratt arising from allegations of speeding against a third party, Brian Rix. Garratt sues Eastmond for assault and battery and Commissioner of Police for false imprisonment. Out of court settlement by Metropolitan Police in sum of £300. No action taken against Eastmond. Wynn-Parry Report on pay and conditions in prison service.

1958 Major street disturbances involving racial violence in Notting Hill and Nottingham in August. Lord Parker succeeds Rayner Goddard as Lord Chief Justice of England, who retires aged 81.

1959 Mental Health Act introduces major reforms in arrangements for the treatment of the mentally ill, including ending of 'legal certification'. Obscene Publications Act reforms law in light of cases such as *The Philanderer* (1954). Chief Constable of Nottingham suspended by Watch Committee following conflict between him and local authority concerning investigation of financial matters affecting the authority. Chief Constable reinstated by Home Secretary. Government White Paper, *Penal Practice in a Changing Society*.

1960 Establishment of Royal Commission on the Police (Chairman Henry Willink, QC), following parliamentary debates on Thurso and Eastmond cases. Makes first report in November on police pay. Publication of first unexpurgated edition of *Lady Chatterley's Lover* in UK. Trial and acquittal of Penguin Books Ltd charged under Obscene Publications Act 1959. Report of the Ingelby Committee on Children and Young Persons. Establishment of Cambridge Institute of Criminology.

1961 Suicide Act makes suicide and attempted suicide no longer crimes.

1962 February–April: trial, appeal and execution of James Hanratty for the murder of Michael Gregsten (the A6 murder). Serious doubts about whether the crime was committed by Hanratty have grown since his death, occasioning books by Louis Blom-Cooper, QC, and Paul Foot. Second Report of the Royal Commission on the Police in May. Dissenting note by Dr Goodhart on the subject of a national police force. First detention centre for girls opens.

1963 Children and Young Persons Act raises age of criminal responsibility to ten years. Harold Wilson sets up working party on criminal justice under chairmanship of the Earl of Longford. Great Train Robbery in August.

1964 Public order disturbed by groups of 'Mods' and 'Rockers' over Easter and Whitsun at various seaside resorts, including Clacton, Margate and Brighton. Publication of Report of Longford Committee, *Crime: A Challenge to Us All*. Police Act. General election in October: Labour government formed with majority of four.

1965 Abolition of Capital Punishment Act. To run for five years and to be affirmed by both Houses of Parliament by 31 July 1970. Vote in House of Commons, 200 to 98 votes. Publication of White Paper, *The Child, the Family and the Young Offender*.

1966 Shooting of George Cornell, gangland associate of the Richardson brothers from South London in *Blind Beggar* public house in Whitechapel in March. Labour returned with Commons majority of 96 in March general election.

1967 Control of Drugs Act to deal with growing abuse of cannabis, amphetamines, LSD and other substances. Road Safety Act introduces 'breathalyser' and sets legal maximum of alcohol for drivers at 80 mg per 100 ml of blood. Criminal Justice Act. First far-reaching and comprehensive reform of sentencing since 1948. Introduces suspended sentences and makes suspension mandatory for sentences of six months or less, thus effectively removing power to imprison from magistrates (later amended following strong pressure from Magistrates' Association). Sexual Offences Act makes homosexual acts between consenting males over 21 years no longer illegal (except in the armed forces). Abortion Act, introduced by David Steel, to permit legalization of abortion in circumstances where medical opinion certifies that continuation of pregnancy would be detrimental to health of mother or where child was likely to be born handicapped. Becomes the basis for abortion on demand embodied in feminist slogan 'a woman's right to choose'.

1968 Theatres Act abolishes censorship of plays by the Lord Chamberlain. Arrest and trial of members of Kray family and their associates for the murders of George Cornell, Jack ('The Hat') McVitie and other serious crimes. Twins Ronnie and Reggie Kray sentenced to life imprisonment and Charles Kray to ten years. A forensic triumph for Detective Chief Inspector 'Nipper' Read of the Metropolitan Police Serious Crimes Squad. Publication of White Paper, *Children in Trouble*. Demonstrations against the war in Indo-China (Vietnam) outside US Embassy in Grosvenor Square involving massive confrontations between crowds and police. Disorders involving students at Paris and other French universities mimicked by students in British Universities involving 'occupations' by students and others of university premises.

1969 Children and Young Persons Act provides for major revision of law relating to juvenile offenders following White Papers, *The Child, the Family and the Young Offender* (1965) and *Children in Trouble* (1968).

1971 Criminal Damage Act. Lord Widgery succeeds Lord Parker as Lord Chief Justice of England.

1974 Following general election of February Labour forms government with Liberal support. Campaign of IRA bombings in mainland UK. Birmingham pub bombing in November. Allegations of unlawful violence by police and prison staff against prisoners who are subsequently sentenced to life imprisonment. Serious doubts about their conviction remain especially in respect of the forensic evidence given at the trial (appeal for a retrial rejected by House of Lords in 1988). Further bombings of pubs in Guildford and Woolwich. Persons subsequently convicted to protest their innocence for the next 14 years. Cases referred to Court of Appeal in January 1989 (on grounds of new evidence) following representations to Home Secretary by Archbishop of Canterbury, Cardinal Archbishop of Westminster, two former Home Secretaries (Roy Jenkins and Merlyn Rees) and two former Lords Justice of Appeal (Scarman and Devlin).

Conflict between protesters and National Front members in Red Lion Square, Holborn, in course of which death of Kevin Gately occurs. Appointment of Lord Scarman to conduct inquiry Conflict between police and pickets during miners' strike outside a coking plant at Saltley, West Midlands.

1977 Mass picketing at Grunwick film processing plant in North London in June and July.

1979 The 'winter of discontent': strikes by transport drivers, public service employees, hospital workers and civil servants from January to March. In March, government loses vote of 'no confidence' by one vote. In May general election, Conservatives under Margaret Thatcher returned with Commons majority of 43. Commons permitted free vote on motion in July to reintroduce the death penalty; defeated by 362 votes to 243. Southall riots and death of Blair Peach.

1980 Lord Lane succeeds Lord Widgery as Lord Chief Justice of England.

1981 Serious rioting in Brixton, South London and Toxteth district of Liverpool. Inquiry into causes conducted by Lord Justice Scarman.

1982 Criminal Justice Bill. Various new clauses introduced at Report stage seeking to restore capital punishment in particular circumstances: all defeated.

1983 Conservatives returned with Commons majority of 166 in June general election. Motion to restore the death penalty for murder defeated by 368 votes to 223 in July. Amendments also defeated. Leon Brittan replaces William Whitelaw at Home Office in October. New severe restrictions on parole leading to case of *Findlay and others* (1984). Mass demonstration of 30,000 women at US Greenham Common missile base in December.

1984 Miners' strike begins in March. Police National Reporting Centre established. Murder of WPC Yvonne Fletcher by unknown gunman firing from Libyan Peoples' Bureau in London in April. In June, serious disorders at Orgreave, South Yorkshire. Complaints of police brutality in using mounted officers against pickets. IRA detonates bomb in Grand Hotel, Brighton, killing four during Conservative Party Conference in October. Thatcher narrowly escapes assassination.

1985 Collapse of miners' strike in March. Serious rioting in Handsworth district of Birmingham in September; two Asians killed. Rioting in Brixton and Toxteth district of Liverpool. Leon Brittan replaced by Douglas Hurd at Home Office. Rioting on Broadwater Farm Estate, Tottenham, North London in October. PC Blakelock killed by rioters.

1987 January: major demonstration at News International plant at Wapping. 162 police casualties and 67 arrests. Third reading of Criminal Justice Bill in April: new clause on death penalty defeated by 342 votes to 230. General election in June: Conservatives returned with Commons majority of 101.

1988 Criminal Justice Bill: new clause introduced on third reading in June to permit juries to recommend death penalty defeated by 123 votes. July: publication of Green Papers on prison privatization and punishment in the community. October: announcement by Lord Chancellor, Lord Mackay of Clashfern of impending Green Paper (1989) on fundamental reform of organization of legal profession.

Select Bibliography

There is a wealth of material relating to British society since 1945 and its very abundance constitutes something of a problem to the student of the period. In a sense it is as well to begin with a political perspective since the shape of society since the end of the Second World War has been definitively moulded by such influences and many of its principal institutions have been shaped – or reshaped – by governments during the post-war years. Peter Hennessy and Anthony Seldon (eds), *Ruling Performance: British Governments from Attlee to Thatcher* (Oxford, Blackwell, 1987) provides an excellent account of the political background to events throughout the period and is especially useful in demonstrating the magnitude of change, not least in the manners of politics between the late 1940s and the late 1980s. Michael Sissons and Philip French (eds), *Age of Austerity: 1945–1951* (Sevenoaks, Hodder and Stoughton, 1963; Harmondsworth, Penguin, 1964) contains a number of essays that exactly catch the mood of the times between the end of the war and the Festival of Britain. A. H. Halsey's *Change in British Society*, published by the Oxford University Press for the Open University Social Sciences Foundation Course, was based upon his Reith Lectures of that title and is now in a third edition (1986). Halsey addresses a range of issues including class, education and social mobility and the basis of social order. Angus Stewart (ed.), *Contemporary Britain* (London, Routledge and Kegan Paul, 1983) covers some of the same ground though with different emphases. Martin Joseph's *Sociology for Everyone* (Cambridge, Polity Press in association with Basil Blackwell, 1986 and 1987), although designed for 'O' and 'A' level students of sociology, is particularly helpful to the interested newcomer to the study of contemporary Britain in the way it presents key social data relevant to a number of central themes including crime and deviance.

There is no single book that provides a general account of all the facts about crime and criminal justice since 1945; still less one that deals comprehensively and chronologically with all the various changes that have taken place in the administration of justice and the penal system in general. Hermann Mannheim's *Social Aspects of Crime in England between the Wars* (London, Allen and Unwin, 1940) is a useful guide to the immediate pre-war situation with regard to crime; his *Group Problems in Crime and Punishment* (London, Routledge and Kegan Paul, 1955) is an enigmatically titled book which does, however, contain some rare and valuable material on wartime crimes such as looting and the black market. For original source material on recorded crime and the sentencing practices of the courts, the reader should consult *Criminal Statistics for England and Wales* (and the corresponding data for Scotland). The statistics are published annually and, although their scope and presentation have undergone a number of changes during the relevant period, contemporary statistics include explanatory notes which make some comparisons possible. *Criminal Statistics* are available in local reference libraries while certain data of a specialist kind may be sometimes available from *Supplementary Statistics* on application to the Home Office.

The Home Office Research and Planning Unit, formerly the Home Office Research Unit, has been publishing survey data in the criminological and penological fields since 1955. The series from 1955 to 1969 contains 13 monographs under the general imprint of *Studies in the Causes of Delinquency and the Treatment of Offenders*, including three of critical importance: Mannheim and Wilkins's work on prediction methods, Wilkins's work on delinquent generations and Gibson and Klein's first monograph on murder. Since 1969, about 100 papers have appeared in the series *Home Office Research Studies*, while 43 papers are available in the *Research and Planning* series. Not all public libraries carry the entire list of titles, but those still in print can be obtained through HMSO bookshops.

The standard work on prisons for the early part of the period is Lionel Fox's *The English Prison and Borstal Systems* (London, Routledge and Kegan Paul, 1952). Fox was the Chairman of the Prison Commission and presents a view of the situation through the eyes of an administrator rather than an external critic. Terence Morris, Pauline Morris and Barbara Barer, *Pentonville: the Sociology of an English Prison* (London, Routledge and Kegan Paul, 1963) was the first ever sociological study of a prison in Britain and describes the social life of a large city prison as it was in the late 1950s and early 1960s. Richard Sparks's *Local Prisons: the Crisis in the English Penal System* (London, Heinemann, 1971) contains much useful material and is important as a prescient statement of what was to become a reality by the end of the decade, albeit that its publication was received like the utterance of a latter-day Cassandra.

On sentencing practices, the literature is again considerable. Sir Leo Page's *The Young Lag* (London, Faber, 1950) is a rare work by a practising judge and an early plea for constructive and consistent sentencing. Barbara Wootton's *Crime and Penal Policy* (London, Allen and Unwin, 1978) reflects in erudite fashion on her 50 years in the courts, on the Advisory Council on the Penal System and on other bodies. It is an important account by one of the most influential figures, both politically and academically, of the period. Frank Pakenham, Earl of Longford, one of the other highly influential and articulate figures of the time, produced *Causes of Crime* (London, Weidenfeld and Nicolson) in 1958. For details of the sentences available to the courts, the Home Office publication, *The Sentence of the Court: a Handbook for Courts on the Treatment of Offenders* (London, HMSO, 1986) sets out in precise detail all the available options. By reference to earlier editions of this handbook it is possible to observe the legislative changes that have taken place with regard to various options for disposal. In this regard, and for a number of other important topics including the parole system, David (Lord) Windlesham's *Responses to Crime* (Oxford, The Clarendon Press, 1987) is a most useful source of information.

For material on policing during the period a distinction must be made between police memoirs and other commentaries. In the former category are to be found Gilbert Kelland, *Crime in London* (London, The Bodley Head, 1986) and Robert Mark's *In the Office of Constable* (London, Collins, 1978). Kelland's book is particularly useful for its perspectives on policing in the immediate post-war period and during the various corruption scandals of the 1960s. Richard Hobbs' *Doing the Business* (Oxford, The Clarendon Press, 1988) is a most useful source for material on the Metropolitan Police, especially on the period of Mark's Commissionership. It is a balancing contrast to passages in David Ascoli's *The Queen's Peace* (London, Hamish Hamilton, 1979), which is a comprehensive history of the Metropolitan Police and contains useful factual material on the period though it is sometimes presented from a partisan viewpoint. In 1983 Simon Holdaway, a former Metropolitan sergeant turned academic, published *Inside the British Police* (Oxford, Blackwell) based on his own fieldwork observations among policemen which is a useful comparison with the earlier work of Maureen Cain, *Society and the Policeman's Role* (London, Routledge and Kegan Paul, 1973). The constitutional position of the police, particularly in respect of social and political accountability is considered in detail in Ian Oliver, *Police, Government and Accountability* (London, MacMillan, 1987). For a distinctive and critical account of recent practical and constitutional issues in policing, including the miners' strike and other public order incidents, Phil Scraton (ed.), *Law, Order and the Authoritarian State: Readings in Critical Criminology* (Oxford, Oxford University Press, 1987) is a highly informative source of factual material. An early study of the police and race relations is to be found in John Lambert, *Crime, Police and Race Relations: a Study in Birmingham* (Oxford, Oxford University Press, 1970).

Source material on the social background to crime and delinquency during the period is comparatively rich. Among works of interest to the new reader, B. M. Spinley, *The Deprived and the Privileged* (London, Routledge and Kegan Paul, 1953) looks at the socialization of children in London, while Madeleine Kerr, *The People of Ship Street* (London, Routledge and Kegan Paul, 1958) examines life in a deprived area of Liverpool. John Mays, *Growing up in the City* (Liverpool, Liverpool University Press, 1954) is a classic work from a master of the period. W. J. H. Sprott, Pearl Jephcott and M. P. Carter, *The Social Background of Delinquency* (Nottingham, University of Nottingham, 1954) looks at the mining village of Hucknall. This seminal work was never commercially published but some specialist libraries such as the British Library of Political and Economic Science possess copies. David Downes's *The Delinquent Solution* (London, Routledge and Kegan Paul, 1966) is a study of crime and delinquency in London's East End; Terence Morris's earlier work, *The Criminal Area* (London, Routledge and Kegan Paul, 1958) examines similar problems in the London borough of Croydon. The numerous criminal biographies of Tony Parker, published in the 1960s, are outstanding contributions to the data on criminals themselves; his *The Frying Pan: a Prison and its Prisoners* (New York, Basic Books, 1970) is a unique account of inmates in the psychiatric prison at Grendon. John McVicar, *McVicar: By Himself* is an unusual and penetrating autobiography of a self-reformed professional criminal (London, Hutchinson, 1974).

The subject of capital punishment, a dominant theme throughout the period, has attracted a large number of polemical works almost without exception in favour of abolition. Louis Blom-Cooper (ed.), *The Hanging Question* (London, Duckworth, 1969) is a good example of the genre. Terence Morris and Louis Blom-Cooper, *A Calendar of Murder* (London, Michael Joseph, 1964) analyses every case of murder indicted in England and Wales from the inception of the Homicide Act of 1957 to the end of 1962. While there is no good commentary on the legislation and various attempts to restore capital punishment subsequent to the 1957 Act, James Christoph's *Capital Punishment and British Politics* (London, Allen and Unwin, 1962) is an invaluable account of events between 1948 and 1957 and is probably the best source, saving *Hansard*, of the minutiae of events in and around Parliament affecting the issue.

Index